JUST BETWEEN FRIENDS

✦ JUST BETWEEN FRIENDS ✦

Women Sharing and Learning Together

✦ COMPILED BY TERRY MEEUWSEN ✦

A JANET THOMA BOOK

THOMAS NELSON PUBLISHERS
Nashville

Scripture quotations noted NKJV are from THE NEW KING JAMES
VERSION. Copyright © 1979, 1980, 1982, 1990,
Thomas Nelson, Inc., Publishers.

Scripture quotations noted NIV are from the
HOLY BIBLE: NEW INTERNATIONAL VERSION®.
Copyright © 1973, 1978, 1984 by International Bible Society.
Used by permission of Zondervan Publishing House. All rights reserved.

Scripture quotations noted TLB are from *The Living Bible,*
copyright © 1971. Used by permission of Tyndale House Publishers, Inc.,
Wheaton, Illinois 60189. All rights reserved.

Somebody Prayed for Me
Words and music by Paul Smith and Dwight Liles
© copyright 1995 Ariose Music (ASCAP). Admin. by EMI
Christian Music Publishing. All rights reserved. Used by permission.

Library of Congress Cataloging-in-Publication Data
Just between friends : women sharing and learning together /
compiled by Terry Meeuwsen.
p.   cm.
ISBN 0-7852-7496-0 (hardcover)
1. Christian women—Religious life. 2. Female friendship—
Religious aspects—Christianity. I. Meeuwsen, Terry Anne.
BV4527.J87   1999
248.8'43—dc21
98-53698
CIP

Printed in the United States of America.
1 2 3 4 5 6 QPK 04 03 02 01 00 99

To my sister, Judie,
who has sacrificially given herself to our friendship
and loved me beyond what I've ever deserved.

♦   ♦   ♦

And to Linda,
who has always been there and who has taught me,
by her example, to be a "balcony friend" and to
listen to the heart-cry of others.

contents

Acknowledgments   IX

Foreword ◆ Twila Paris   XI

Time Stood Still ◆ *Terry Meeuwsen*   1

Part One: moments of Sharing

Welcome Home, Jenny ◆ *Terry Meeuwsen*   5

Twin Pots ◆ *Patsy Clairmont*   9

When the Gift Is the Giver ◆ *Stormie Omartian*   12

Press On ◆ *Terry Meeuwsen*   17

Of Kindred Spirits ◆ *Ruth J. Ruibal*   21

I'll Meet You at the Gate ◆ *Linda Strom*   25

Through Thick and Thin ◆ *Marilyn Hickey*   31

Lessons in Togetherness ◆ *Out of Eden*   35

From Bows to Butter Roses ◆ *Vonette Bright*   39

A Polite but Distant Smile ◆ *Karen Mains*   42

Where Two Are Gathered ◆ *Lynn Hallimore*   46

Part two: moments of Diversity

Just As We Are ◆ *Terry Meeuwsen*   53

Beyond the Blue ◆ *Pam Mellskog*   57

Not Too Far from Here ◆ *Kim Boyce*   61

The Language of Girlfriends ◆ *Chonda Pierce*   65

The Greeks Have Stolen My Heart ◆ *Luci Swindoll*   70

The Odd Couple ◆ *Madeline Manning Mims*   75

PART THREE: MOMENTS OF CHILDHOOD FRIENDSHIP

No Work, No Play! ✦ *Terry Meeuwsen*   81
Willie Mae ✦ *Cathy Riso*   83
The Move to Mars and Venus ✦ *Cathy Lechner*   88
Sunday Sister ✦ *Carol Cymbala*   94
Can You Reach My Friend? ✦ *Sara White*   97

PART FOUR: MOMENTS OF COMFORT

Aunt Linda ✦ *Terry Meeuwsen*   103
A Gift Beyond Measure ✦ *Linda Strom*   107
Ordinary People ✦ *Lee Ezell*   110
The Unfinished Conversation ✦ *Evelyn Roberts*   117
Judy to the Rescue ✦ *Liz Curtis Higgs*   121
The Six-Week Sacrifice ✦ *Terry Dorian*   124
Lifelong Friendship ✦ *Terry Meeuwsen*   129

acknowledgments

he adage, "Many hands make light work," rings true for this book, which did indeed require many hands. Thank you to all of my friends who readily and enthusiastically contributed their heartfelt stories. You are special ladies. Thanks to Janet Thoma for direction, encouragement, and her uncompromising commitment to excellence. I also want to mention a special thank you to Debbie Eicholtz, whose design work added such warmth, beauty, and nostalgia to this project.

A friend who isn't written about in this book but without whom the book wouldn't exist is Rhonda Palser, my assistant. The truth is, my entire schedule would cease to function without her. She has walked hand in hand with me through this venture. Though it has meant considerably more work for her, she encouraged me to go forward with the book, and then she tackled the ensuing challenges with gusto. There isn't a page that hasn't been touched in some way by her. Rhonda's quiet, gentle spirit and ready smile are blessings I don't take for granted. Her friendship is icing on the cake.

I also want to thank my husband, Andy, and our four children, Drew, Tory, J. P., and Tyler. Andy, for understanding that many nights my ability to write in peace didn't begin until 11:00 P.M. and could stretch into the wee hours. He never complained. And my children, for understanding that Mom's "homework" had due dates too.

While so many people long to find a good friend, I feel abundantly blessed to have so many wonderful women who have touched my life with their gift of friendship. Many of you, dear friends, will not find your names here because of the project's boundaries. Please know how valuable your friendships are to me and how much they have shaped and blessed my life. I thank the Lord for each and every one of you.

foreword

It's wonderful to have many friends, but we all need a few really close, intimate friends around us—the kind who seem to have been called by God to seek us out when we need them, to encourage us, and to comfort us. We relax into their company like an easy chair. They love us for who we are, and they love us enough to be honest about whom we need to be. Some friends are with us throughout our lives, and some appear for just a season but leave a permanent addition to our hearts.

The very best friends are the ones who simply inspire us to be more like Jesus. Terry Meeuwsen is that kind of friend. I like a lot of things about her, but what I like most is that her passion for God is contagious. Just by being herself she consistently says or does something that challenges me to grow in my relationship with God. I am grateful to call Terry my friend, along with many of the women she has gathered to contribute to this book.

I encourage you, as you read their stories, to remember to thank God for the friends He has given you. May you find a new determination to be the friend He calls you to be and may you always be blessed with the kind of friendship this book reminds us to pursue.

—*Twila Paris,* Singer, Songwriter

terry meeuwsen

time stood still

grew up in a small town just outside of Green Bay, Wisconsin. In our town everybody knew everybody, which was sometimes a blessing and sometimes a challenge. Most families have lived there for at least a couple of generations. The businesses were family owned and operated. Friendships that began in grade school lasted a lifetime. Doctors made house calls, neighbors knew each other, and children played kick-the-can long after dark. In Wisconsin, we weren't paying close attention while Peter, Paul, and Mary were harmonizing "The Times They Are A-Changin'." We should have listened.

By the time we reached the '90s, we had become enmeshed in frenzied schedules and technological advances that allowed us to do business without meeting face-to-face. While we've added complexity, it has detracted from our relationships. Like you, I have to make a concerted effort to nurture my friendships. Other things in life—family, business, ministry—tend to eat up the hours in a day.

Another '90s reality is that geographical distance often separates us from special people near to our hearts. Yet the moment we connect with those friends by phone or in person, we seem to pick up right where we left off . . . almost as though, when it came to our friendship, time stood still.

Friendship's special bond has a resiliency that even we who experience it can't explain. It's a strength that withstands time and stress. And it strengthens us. At the end of a long day or in the midst of the chaos of it all, we are bolstered when we receive an unexpected card that says, "I'm thinking of you" or a reassuring phone message of "You're on my heart." A fax or an e-mail may also transmit a friend's caring message.

In that moment, whether I'm sending or receiving, I feel a stirring in my heart, a smile comes to my lips, and I'm aware of what a special gift that friend is. Often God has spoken to me, comforted me, encouraged me, or even exhorted me through a friend's loving heart.

This book is a tribute to those special people in our lives whose unconditional love and selfless caring have enriched us beyond measure. Women from a variety of seasons in life have contributed their memories of moments with friends from long ago or here and now. Some of the women are well-known, others are not; some are young, others are older; some have known great wealth, others live simple lives. But each holds two things in common: a love for the Lord and a love for her best friend.

And I know their stories will remind you of a memorable experience with your friends, so throughout the book you will find special pages to record those memories—either to save for yourself or to give this book to a friend.

So find a cozy chair and snuggle in to read. You'll experience afresh friendship moments of your own as the women who have contributed their stories tell of moments of sharing, moments of diversity (friends who seemingly are mismatched), moments of childhood friendship, and moments of comfort or encouragement. As you read each section and each story, revel with these women in the joy we can share over one of God's most precious gifts: our cherished friends.

Part One

✦ moments of sharing ✦

The bag lady; my cousin, Connie; my sister, Judie;
my cousin's daughter, Chelsea; my daughter, Tory; and
Connie's youngest daughter, Taylor; greet Jenny at the airport.

terry meeuwsen

welcome home, jenny

’m sometimes inhibited in public. Because of that, I'm fascinated by people who aren't. My sister, Judie, and my cousin, Connie Sabo, are two of the funniest, most uninhibited people I know. They share a very special friendship, and when I'm with them, the joy of their relationship spills over onto me. I expect to laugh when we're together.

They do things I would never do. Once they went to an amusement park with a studio in which a person can make her own music video. You choose a music track and lip-synch, play instruments, and dance to the tune of your choice. Afterward, you walk away with a video of your performance. While you're doing all this, mind you, a crowd gathers outside the viewing window to watch. I would die a thousand torturous deaths before I would do such a thing. Not Judie and Connie! They really got into it. With eyes closed, they boogied and sang their little hearts out. My kids think Aunt Judie and Aunt Connie are the best.

Several years ago, our three families established a tradition of spending Thanksgiving together. Judie and her family come to my home in Virginia Beach from Charlotte, N.C., while Connie and her family come from Atlanta. During these holiday get-togethers, the kids write and perform talent shows that leave us aching from laughter and tears. We've played charades until we couldn't mime one more thought or make one more wild guess. Our Thanksgiving meal is a generous and memorable combination of all of our recipes and traditions. It's a special time of sharing friendship and the joy of being together.

Last fall, my sister's oldest child, Jennifer, left to attend college at the University of Central Florida. She would arrive last at our Thanksgiving fest. Feeling pretty special as the only college student in the group and returning to the fold for the first time, she announced to her mom she hoped a welcoming committee would greet her at the airport. We all determined to give her a welcome she would long remember. The dads decided to hold down the fort, which roughly translated meant watch a football game together. That left the three of us and our children for the trip to the airport.

Judie and Connie decided each person would create a unique outfit. We unpacked masks from storage boxes, and Dr. Seuss hats from closet shelves. Zany sunglasses and crazy clothing were donned by all. Then the poster board and markers came out for signs that read "Welcome home, Jenny" and other expressions from the heart.

The Norfolk airport is a small, user-friendly airport so a group like ours would not go unnoticed. As I contemplated our little endeavor, I remembered a large back-lit picture of Pat Robertson and me on the studio set welcoming all arrivals to the Tidewater area and inviting them to visit *The 700 Club*. It sits right above the escalator that takes arriving passengers to baggage claim.

Oh, my word! I can't go to the airport and make an idiot of myself, I decided. *Someone will recognize me and think I'm crazy!*

That's when the paper bag first came to mind. It seemed perfect. By cutting two holes for my eyes, I could enjoy the event but remain totally anonymous. My eight-year-old son teased me about being a bag lady, and I laughed with him. This costume suited me just fine.

I can't tell you how liberating it was to be incognito. We entered the airport looking like the Beverly Hillbillies, but I felt unfazed and a little like the invisible man.

Jen's plane finally arrived, and as she walked toward us, we whooped and hollered and totally decimated any collegiate *savoir faire* she may have been trying to exhibit. It was a wonderful moment to share with Judie and Connie, but I was thankful for the all-enveloping brown bag, determined to keep it on until I reached the car.

In the close quarters of the baggage claim area, I began to feel a little more self-conscious about my "getup." Nervous self-talk danced through my head. *Just a few more minutes, and I'll be out of here. Thank heavens I don't see anyone I know.*

"Mom, you can take the bag off now!" My eight year old couldn't appreciate my need for anonymity, so he yanked the paper bag off my head.

Before I could respond to my "unveiling," I felt a hand on my arm, and a woman I'd never laid eyes on before whispered into my ear, "I just *love* your show!"

Judie, Connie, and I have shared loads of laughter through the years as well as heartfelt discussions about life's challenges and spiritual truths. Not the least of which is that an inhibited person should never go to the airport with a bag over her head accompanied by her eight-year-old son!

In the following stories, other women tell of friends who shared special moments with them. Some of the times were zany; some were sorrowful. But the one constant was a friend who laughed, listened, loved, prayed, and counseled when exuberance, advice, or solace was needed. For true sisterhood is built on the ability to confide in one another.

And, true friendship is also built on accountability. True friends help us to see ourselves honestly, stand with courage in the midst of difficulties, and cling to the Lord when we can't see clearly. For such moments, we need our friends.

Patsy Clairmont shares tea with her friend Carol.

◆ ◆ ◆

"The language of friendship
is not words but meaning."
—Henry David Thoreau

Patsy CLairmont

twin pots

n an antique-shopping excursion, my friend Carol spotted a teapot with an illustration of two girls holding hands. She purchased it for me. Several months later, while once again browsing for treasures, Carol discovered a duplicate pot. This one, she bought for herself. Our twin pots have become a hallmark of our valued, forty-year friendship.

In many ways Carol and I are twin pots. (At this season, even our shapes are more, shall we say, *pottish* looking than in our youth.) And we both spout off from time to time—but only with the warmest of intentions.

Carol and I have always enjoyed each other's company, and we share many common interests. We love to chatter about decorating, to study and critique art pieces, to discover antiques, to experience varied dining establishments (especially tea rooms), and to laugh until tears of joy leave us in soggy relief.

Through the years Carol and I have spent time away at cottages and bed-and-breakfast accommodations seeking solace and sanity from life's mercurial ways. At the end of such weeks, our husbands join us, and we conclude our adventure as a foursome.

Often Carol, an artist by trade, will sketch a picture of something in our new surroundings, and I will write a poem to go with the sketch. At a beautiful inn near Lake Michigan, I found myself drawn to a statue at the edge of a pool beside a meadow. It was of a young boy playing a harp. Carol captured the boy with her pencil. Then early one morning over breakfast tea I penned:

> *Meadow boy, come out to play,*
> *Symphony of breaking day.*
> *Child of wonder, child of song,*
> *To us alone this place belongs.*
> *Harp of stone, hymn of praise,*
> *noted songs in morning rays.*
> *Sing to heaven songs of earth,*
> *minstrel joy and floral mirth.*

We tuck these sketches and poems into our journals as memory-enhancers for the time when we'll be too old to travel and will be relegated to twin, motorized rocking chairs. These personal treasures help us to capture a sense of the places we have visited, the people we have met, and the lessons we have learned. And if we have figured out one thing in our journey, it's that life is full of lessons.

I am a lesson all by myself—there are several people who would confirm this. I have established a reputation for being a cracked pot. Carol, too, is a flawed pot, but we both long to be restored and used as worthy vessels. (Maybe even soothing teapots!) Our twin desire for restoration, linked with our willingness to own up to our weaknesses, has allowed us to come alongside each other to offer a hand.

We have discovered many women relate to feeling fragile and broken. Yet we girls (I love that youthful term) are finding we are strengthened when we are honest with each other and receive one another—cracks, chips, and all.

Carol and I know the worst and the best about each other. We are thrilled when one of us succeeds, and we are saddened when one of us experiences failure. We are committed to each other's best and leave room for those invariable times when we let the other down. We, like the twin pot girls, are determined to hold hands no matter how steamed we might become or how hot life's water may be.

Carol and I have dedicated ourselves to appreciating and applauding each other's talents, and to confessing our weakest traits to one another. This mutuality has taken us from the tea parlor where we have shared in life, to the funeral parlor where we have shared in death.

Three years ago, Carol's son Jeff died. I extended a hand of compassion, and we held on for dear life during the waves of grief. How precious we are to each other and how much we need one another!

Eventually Carol and I were able to leave the place of grief and reenter the tea parlor. Sometimes our tea is mixed with tears and sometimes it is sweetened with memories. We are warmed by the tea and by the dear embrace of our friendship.

patsy clairmont

BEST-SELLING AUTHOR OF SUCH BOOKS AS *sportin' a 'tude, under his wings,* AND *god uses cracked pots,* PATSY TRAVELS THROUGHOUT THE COUNTRY SPEAKING AT CONFERENCES, INCLUDING THE WOMEN OF FAITH CONFERENCES. IN ADDITION TO SPRINKLING HUMOR LIKE CONFETTI THROUGHOUT HER TALKS AND WRITINGS, SHE ENJOYS GARDENING AT HER HOME IN BRIGHTON, MICHIGAN. PATSY AND HER HUSBAND, LES, HAVE TWO GROWN SONS. THIS STORY WAS ORIGINALLY PUBLISHED IN THE BOOK, *tea with patsy clairmont.* FROM *tea with patsy clairmont,* © 1997 BY PATSY CLAIRMONT. PUBLISHED BY SERVANT PUBLICATIONS, BOX 8617, ANN ARBOR, MICHIGAN, 48107. USED WITH PERMISSION.

STORMIE OMARTIAN

WHEN THE GIFT IS THE GIVER

used to think I was a generous person. That is, until I met Patti. I was introduced to her when I did a radio interview for a Christian organization where she worked part-time. She was gracious, helpful, supportive, and put me at ease immediately. It was impossible not to love her. As we talked briefly after the program, we discovered we attended the same church and our daughters were the same age. Yet in a congregation of twelve thousand with multiple church services, our paths had never crossed.

I saw more of Patti after our young daughters began to attend the same elementary school. We would wave to one another in the parking lot or call out greetings in the schoolyard, but I didn't really get to know her until after I had major surgery.

A number of wonderful women at the church had arranged to bring food to our family every night for three weeks after I returned home from the hospital. I had never experienced that kind of care before, and I was touched by it. My young children would surely have starved, or we would have eaten pizza every night for three weeks, if it weren't for the sacrifices of these thoughtful ladies.

After the fifth night, I received a call from Patti, who was to deliver dinner. "I need to come over early, if that's all right with you," she said. "I have a lot of things to unload."

"You do? What kind of dinner is this?" I asked.

"Oh, it's not one dinner, it's five," she answered in a way that let me know she didn't think this was out of the ordinary. "And I have some things to occupy your time while you're recovering."

"Come whenever is convenient for you," I said. "I'm definitely not going anywhere in the near future."

"I'll be there at two this afternoon."

That was a full three hours before any of the other women had arrived. I wondered if it was going to take that long to unload her car.

When my doorbell rang at 2:00 P.M., I hobbled slowly to the front door. Patti's arms were filled with a stack of freezer cartons so I pointed her toward the kitchen.

"What have you done, Patti?" I exclaimed. "How much food have you brought?"

"Oh, this is just the beginning," she said with a laugh. "This isn't even all of the first meal."

I glanced at her car and couldn't believe what I saw. It was filled with freezer cartons and cardboard boxes piled high.

"Patti, this isn't *all* for me, is it?" I said, certain she would say no.

"Oh, yes, it is. It's everything a person needs to get well," she replied over her shoulder as she headed toward the kitchen.

I apologized for being unable to help her carry anything in and called my husband, who was working in the studio off the garage, to come and assist her. It must have taken him ten trips to her car before everything was inside. He was as amazed as I was to see what she had done.

"All the elements of each dinner go together, and they are number coded," she explained after everything was stacked in the kitchen. "For example, dinner number one has a chicken dish, a vegetable dish, a potato dish, homemade bread, and a dessert. So these five cartons with the number one on them all go together."

"Homemade bread?" I repeated in astonishment. "You made homemade bread?"

"Oh, yes, and here is the jam to go with it," she said as she searched one of the boxes.

"Oh, good!" I sighed. "I was so worried you might have forgotten something."

She laughed confidently. "Number two is the lamb dinner, and here are the vegetables that go with it, and this is the rice dish. That container holds the blackberry cobbler, and here are the homemade rolls."

"Homemade rolls? You actually prepared homemade rolls? And homemade blackberry cobbler?"

She laughed again and continued on and on until she had explained each dinner.

I noticed on the labels of each container she had written instructions for the oven's temperature, how long the food should cook, which container to put in the oven first, and when to put the others in so everything would be synchronized.

After she had put the food away, she started to unpack the boxes but stopped and said, "Let me take all this into your bedroom. That's probably where you'll be using it."

I slowly led the way.

"These are my favorite magazines, books, and videos," she said of the stacks she laid neatly next to my night table. "Each one is uplifting, and I know you'll love them. Here is some body lotion and Chap Stick. I know how dry your skin can get after surgery. And these are great tapes of worship songs and a few of my favorite teachings on the Bible. I also brought a tape recorder in case you didn't have one small enough to fit on your nightstand." She went on to give a detailed explanation of every item.

When she was done, I laughed even though it hurt to do so. "I don't believe you, Patti. How in the world did you ever find time to do all this? Are you Superwoman or an angel?"

"Oh, I just prepared an especially nice meal for my family every night for the past five nights, and doubled the portions so I could freeze half for you. As for the rest of it, I simply went through my house and gathered all the things I love and thought you might enjoy."

"I'm overwhelmed. How can I ever repay you or thank you for all that you've done?"

"Seeing your joy is reward enough for me," she said and then hugged me good-bye.

Over the next few days we ate every wonderful bite of the food she had made. Over the next few weeks, I enjoyed all the items she had brought. Over the next few months, Patti and I became the best of friends, and so did our daughters.

But the most amazing part of this story is that was only the beginning. Patti's generosity hasn't decreased in all these years. She has taught me what friendship and sacrificial giving truly mean, and I'm still her student to this day.

STORMIE OMARTIAN

STORMIE HAS WRITTEN EIGHT BOOKS INCLUDING *THE POWER OF A PRAYING WIFE, THE POWER OF A PRAYING PARENT,* AND *THAT'S WHAT LOVE IS FOR.* SHE HAS MADE FIVE EXERCISE VIDEOS, TWO OF WHICH SOLD SUFFICIENT COPIES TO BE DECLARED "GOLD." STORMIE HAS BEEN MARRIED FOR TWENTY-FIVE YEARS TO RECORD PRODUCER MICHAEL OMARTIAN, WHO HAS WORKED WITH 4HIM, MICHAEL BOLTON, AMY GRANT, AND DONNA SUMMER. THEY HAVE THREE CHILDREN, INCLUDING ONE SON WHO BECAME PART OF THEIR FAMILY AFTER HIS PARENTS DIED. THE FAMILY RESIDES IN BRENTWOOD, TENNESSEE.

My friend Ruth Ruibal
with her husband, Julio, and daughters,
Sarah and Abigail.

TERRY MEEUWSEN

PRESS ON

first met Ruth when she was my guest on *The 700 Club*. As usual, I had received a fact sheet the night before to give me a bit of background. Ruth's story touched my heart. She and her husband, Julio, were missionaries and pastored a church in Cali, Colombia. God began to speak to Julio about the significance of unity in the body of Christ, and so Julio worked toward that goal. Different denominations caught the vision and rose above their differences. In unity they began to gather together by tens of thousands in an outdoor arena for all-night prayer vigils. They prayed for unity and for God to move on their city's behalf to end the Mafia-like influence of the drug cartel. As they prayed, the tightly run cartel began to unravel.

Eventually, Julio was shot and killed outside the church as a warning to those who would interfere with the cartel. His American wife and two daughters were left to carry on.

What would they do? I was curious to meet this woman who had been widowed just months before.

"Are you afraid to stay and carry on?" I asked.

"Since Julio's death, we have seen even greater unity among the pastors of Cali," she answered. "The Spirit of God is moving

✦ 17

powerfully. What the enemy meant for evil, God is using to bring about good, just as He promised."

"What about the girls? Do they want to stay?"

"When I was told that Julio had been shot, I rushed to the church. Sarah, our youngest, had been with Julio and was sitting on the sidewalk next to his body. Her first question was, 'Does this mean we have to go back to America?' You see, our daughters have watched as God has moved in Cali. They have prayed with us for this outpouring of His Spirit. Though Julio died for the sake of the gospel, we don't want to miss seeing what God will do. This is what we have worked for."

I was deeply moved. No pity, no discouragement, no fear showed on Ruth's face nor in her voice.

Since we first met, our friendship has grown. I have learned many things from Ruth. Her devotion to the Lord exceeds the unexpected tragedies in her life. You see, she not only lost Julio but also her mother and her best friend within six months of Julio's death. (She tells her story on page 21.) Yet Ruth presses on. How? By pressing in close to the only One who can fill our souls and mend our broken hearts. She has taught me that when it's time to press on, we need to press in!

✦ ✦ ✦

"A true friend advises justly,
assists readily, adventures boldly, takes all
patiently, defends courageously, and
continues a friend unchangeably."
— William Penn

true friends

I REMEMBER WHEN WE MET . . .

_____

_____

_____

_____

◆　◆　◆

TOGETHER WE HAVE SHARED OUR LOVE OF . . .

_____

_____

_____

_____

◆　◆　◆

I THANK YOU FOR ALLOWING ME TO SHARE YOUR
LIFE, PARTICULARLY THIS TIME WHEN I FELT SO CLOSE
TO YOU:

_____

_____

_____

_____

Ruth Ruibal and daughters with Diana Evernden

♦ ♦ ♦

"Friends are great long-range lookers—
they see what you can become and gently
prod you in that direction."
—Unknown

RutH J. RuIBaL

of kindred spirits

t was a cool morning in the spring of 1984 at the
Weimar Institute in the mountains of northern
California where I was taking a live-in health
course. Little did I realize that a most treasured
friendship was about to develop.

Each morning eight of us would eat breakfast together. On this
morning a new woman sat at our table. Diana Evernden was tall,
well dressed, and stately. She was a bit older than I and seemed to
be very proper, which made me a bit uncomfortable. As we all
talked, we discovered she had attended the first session that year
and had returned for some additional time. Diana was suffering
from a congenital heart condition that hadn't been discovered until
she was about forty years of age.

After breakfast each person had her schedule planned. Some went
to hydrotherapy, others to exercise class, and others walked the trails
through the woods. Today, as we discussed our schedules, Diana and
I were the only ones whose walking schedule coincided. Although I
wasn't too keen about spending the morning with someone with
whom I felt uncomfortable, I quickly prayed to myself, *Lord, it seems
this is ordained of You. So I will use this opportunity to speak to Diana*

about You. She needs a special touch in light of the seriousness of her physical condition.

So Diana and I took off for the hills. Her first question was, "What do you do?"

"My husband and I live in Cali, Colombia, with our two girls. We're missionaries."

"Oh, really? What church are you with?"

"We're Christians but don't represent any particular denomination." And so the conversation took off. To my surprise, Diana was also a Christian and interested in mission work.

That weekend her husband, Tom, came to visit, and the three of us spent some time together walking and talking about the things of God. Some weeks later, my husband, Julio, came to finish the last couple of days of the session with me, and the four of us hit it off. After the session, Diana and Tom invited us to stop by their home in California for a few days. We did, and our friendship began to deepen as Julio and I shared our vision for what the Lord would do in Cali. Diana and Tom believed with us for the invisible as if it were already visible. Our lives became united with the desire to see the Word of the Lord come into its fullness.

By the end of the trip, Diana and Tom committed themselves to provide housing, food, and transportation any time we were in the area. We also agreed that, although they might feel led to help with financial support for the work from time to time, they would not give us any personal financial support. That allowed our friendship to grow without economics interfering with the special relationship God was establishing.

The following year, when we were back in the area, the Lord led us to start the Julio C. Ruibal Foundation. Our first official address was the Evernden home, and Diana was the first secretary-treasurer. I can't describe what it meant to us to have someone believe and see when nothing was visible to the natural eye.

The next year, Diana and Tom visited us in Cali. Our college had just started, and Diana, an interior decorator and artist, helped set up the classrooms and dormitory.

As the years went on, Diana and I shared a close relationship. She was the kind of friend whom I could call at any time for any problem or just to say "hi". No matter what the situation was, she had the wonderful capacity of seeing Jesus in it. We would talk every month or two, but our relationship was always warm and encouraging. I could speak into her life and she into mine. As Diana would say, "We're of kindred spirits." I always knew she was there for me and my family.

One time our families spent ten days together. By then our two girls, Sarah and Abigail, had asked Tom if he would be their grandfather since my own father had died just after Abigail's birth. Tom and Diana took us to their cabin in California's redwoods. What a blessed time we had sharing our lives and the Lord with one another. The woods were so tranquil, especially to our family since we had just come from so much violence, crime, and drug trafficking in Cali.

The stream behind the cabin was like crystal. We walked through the woods, picked berries, cooked, talked, played around the fireplace, and had one of the most wonderful times we could remember.

As the Lord blessed our work, the invisible things Diana and I had spoken about over the years became visible. And the Everndens rejoiced with us. But along with the blessings came the spiritual warfare. Our lives were threatened.

My mother was elderly by then, and I didn't feel free to share with her about the serious danger we were facing. But I had Diana, who could listen and confirm that we are safe only when we are in the center of God's will, no matter how difficult or dangerous the situation.

During the summer of '95, the threats against Julio's life increased. Diana was always there on the other end of the phone to believe, pray with me, and encourage me. She was a true friend who never was an alarmist, never seemed to be frightened by the circumstances, and always pointed me to Jesus.

During the first few days of September, I wanted to call her. I felt a deep emotional pain, something I had never experienced before. I told Julio about it and was concerned that perhaps it was because my mother was dying. I never did call Diana.

The following week, her oldest daughter phoned to say Diana had gone to be with the Lord. What a shock and what deep pain and grief. When I heard the news I knew this was what I had been feeling. My loss was more than I can describe. I knew I would probably never have another friendship like hers.

Some months later, God drew forty-five thousand Christians to a stadium to pray all night for our city. The Christians were united and praying—and the Cali cartel was falling apart. At the same time the threats continued against Julio's life. Then, on December 13, Julio was shot by a hit man.

I was suddenly a widow whose best friend had died just months before. The only solace I found was in Jesus. Had Diana, my kindred spirit, been there, I probably would have relied on her when the Lord wanted me to rely on Him. Now I can say, He does everything well.

RUTH RUIBAL

RUTH moved to Cali, Colombia, after she graduated with a master's degree from Columbia University. She taught in Colombia's state university master's program. In 1973 she served as a consultant for the Pan American Health Organization/World Health Organization. At that time she met Julio Ruibal, and they were married in 1976. Ruth and her daughters (now teenagers) remain based in Cali where they are active in ministry.

LINDA STROM

I'LL meet you at the gate

t 5:30 P.M. on February 3, 1998, I was brought face-to-face with time in a way I had never experienced it. A flood of sadness rushed toward me as I hurried to the chapel at Mountain View Prison in Gatesville, Texas. I was aware of how fleeting time is and how it can simultaneously stand still. I had asked my precious friend, Karla Tucker Brown, what she would like me to do on February 3, the day of her execution. Her reply had been quick, soft, and yet passionate. "I'd like you to tell the women here that God is with me. He's the same in the hard times as in the good times."

Since eleven that morning I had walked with several friends throughout that prison, telling the women just what Karla Faye had requested. Hearts were open and ready to hear that Jesus had paid the penalty for Karla's sins, for mine, and for theirs. Miracles often occur at the most unlikely times, and on that beautiful sunny Texas day, hearts were awakened to Jesus' love even as Karla went to be with Him.

In the months before the execution, I had reflected on how my unique friendship with Karla Faye had emerged. As my husband, Dallas, once tearfully asked as he contemplated Karla's death, "How did we get here?"

I first met Karla Faye more than a decade ago. I had walked from the chapel to death row at Gatesville, a little anxious about this opportunity to share Christ's love with the women there. I was exhausted, as I had just finished leading a weekend prison seminar. Sleeping had been a challenge the night before. Yet I desperately wanted God to give me words of life.

As I approached death row, I saw Karla and she was smiling. She had long, curly, brown hair and dark eyes that flashed with excitement. Introducing herself, she gave me a warm hug and then started to ask questions about what had happened at the chapel seminar. Soon I forgot I was on death row and instead felt I was visiting an interested friend. During that time, Karla told me how they had changed the name of death row to *life row* because four women were there, and each had come to know the life talked about in John— the abundant life.

After several hours of meaningful conversation, I had to leave. We prayed and hugged one another. I knew I'd be back.

As I walked to the chapel, I could see Karla Faye at the window. She was smiling as she waved and threw kisses. I walked quickly to a private office, closed the door, and wept. This didn't make sense. Here was one so in love with Jesus, transformed by His grace and power, yet confined with a death sentence.

Over the next ten years I would have many heart-to-heart visits with my friend Karla. We had the same passion for hurting women, and that created a bond between us. Her childhood had been painful, as had mine. We grew in our friendship, and we honestly confronted issues that surface when a person comes face-to-face with truth. We talked vulnerably about anger and lack of forgiveness. As my life was being pruned, so was hers.

Karla was a writer and I looked forward to her long, descriptive letters. I sent pictures of my family, and in one of her letters she wrote of holding those pictures in her hands as she prayed for us. She prayed daily for our ministry and even sent support from her meager account.

I grew to love her like a daughter. Just as our family photo was with her in the death row cell, so was her picture in our home.

In November 1997 Warden Pamela Baggett called to tell me of Karla's date with death since Karla listed me as her spiritual adviser. In reality I was to learn much about joy and surrender through her. I spent hours with her during the next two months. We cried and shared hopes and dreams. But Christ was always our focus.

On one of my last visits, Karla had joy in her face but tears in her eyes. She said, "Linda, I'll be waiting for you by the gate. See you when you get there."

The last time Dallas and I saw Karla was on February 1. We shared communion with her. Then we slowly and peacefully read Psalm 23 and sang "Thou Art Worthy," the song Karla requested. Although we were separated by bars, we still were able to interlock our fingers as we sang. Our fingers ached from the metal mesh, but it was such a gift—that gift of touch.

Then a guard reluctantly walked toward us. With compassion, she quietly told us our time was up. Karla Faye and I placed our faces to the bars, touched cheeks, kissed each other, and said, "I love you." Slowly she and I turned and walked our separate ways, knowing the next time we would meet would be at heaven's gate.

During those last weeks of her life, Karla had a bride's radiance. Each morning as I had walked and prayed before I went to the prison, I had known I was to release Karla to her Bridegroom—but it was difficult.

On Tuesday morning, February 3, before I honored Karla's request to go to the people in prison, I read Revelation 19:1, 7–9:

Hallelujah!
Salvation and glory and power belong to our God . . .
Let us rejoice and be glad
and give him glory!
For the wedding of the Lamb has come,
and his bride has made herself ready.

Fine linen, bright and clean, was given her to wear . . .
Blessed are those who are invited to the wedding supper
of the Lamb! (NIV)

In a sense I had been part of the bridal party.

The hour of the execution was set for 6:00 P.M. A number of women were singing with me at the service in the chapel at Gatesville. Karla loved to sing. But that evening she was two hundred miles away in Huntsville where the execution was to take place. Was she singing with us?

At 6:45 P.M., the telephone rang in the chaplain's office. We were singing the "Battle Hymn of the Republic." As the chaplain at Huntsville announced Karla's home-going, I felt such relief. All I could say was, "Thank You, Father. My friend Karla, the beautiful bride, is safely home."

Later I learned, after she was strapped onto the gurney and said her final words of love, thanks, and a brief appeal for forgiveness, she had concluded with, "I'm going to be face-to-face with Jesus now." And then she sang, probably just at the time we were singing in the chapel at Gatesville.

Two months later I revisited *life row*. A poster hanging on the wall was of Karla Faye—laughing. There were wonderful memories. That day, as I walked back to the chapel, I lifted my eyes toward heaven and said, "I'll meet you at the gate, Karla."

Linda Strom

Linda and her husband, Dallas, founded Discipleship Unlimited, a ministry "for the equipping of the saints" (Eph. 4:12). Together they teach others how to conduct marriage seminars, hold weekly Bible studies, and coordinate volunteer ministries to inmates in prisons. They live in Milwaukee and have three sons and one grandson.

Linda Strom will always remember Karla Tucker Brown, who taught her so much about joy and surrender.

HEART-TO-HEART

CB

TRUE FRIENDS HONESTLY CONFRONT ISSUES THAT SURFACE WHEN A PERSON COMES face-to-face WITH THE TRUTH. THEY TALK VULNERABLY ABOUT ANGER AND LACK OF FORGIVENESS. THEIR LIVES ARE PRUNED AS THEY GROW AND LEARN TOGETHER.

I REMEMBER WHEN MY LIFE WAS BEING PRUNED, AND SO WAS YOURS. WE WERE GROWING AND LEARNING TOGETHER . . .

_____

_____

_____

_____

_____

_____

Marilyn and her husband, Pastor Wallace Hickey,
celebrate with Mary Smith.

♦ ♦ ♦

If you love someone you will be loyal to him no
matter what the cost. You will always believe in
him, always expect the best of him, and always
stand your ground in defending him.
—1 Corinthians 13:7 TLB

THROUGH THICK AND THIN

met Mary Smith probably twenty-four years ago, when the ministry I was beginning was very small—one volunteer, a cardboard box, and a kitchen table in a Sunday school classroom. Mary told me she had been Oral Roberts' second secretary and had worked off and on through the years with him. She wondered if she could help my ministry. Since her husband had become the associate pastor to work alongside my husband at our church, it seemed to fit together nicely.

Then one Sunday morning we had an evangelist speak at our church who asked people to come forward if they felt called to stand with those of us who were ministering. I will never forget that morning. Mary came to stand with me. I knew then that God's Spirit had bonded her to my heart.

Mary was an inspiration because she believed God had called me and that the ministry would grow. Sometimes she believed it more than I did. After all, a pastor's wife having radio and television appearances was unheard of and not well accepted. That never seemed to frighten Mary or put her off.

When the ministry began to grow a little, she had an unusual sensitivity about who was right to hire and who was not. Sometimes the Lord would wake her in the night with ideas for working with our staff, or with insights on how a certain ministry could be done in a more creative way.

Her own children weren't serving God at that time, and yet she took a great interest in mine; she prayed with me, stood in faith with me, and sometimes even cried with me.

I remember one time when she had a blood clot, and the doctors thought she would die. I was in a hotel in Bakersfield, California, when I received the call from her. We prayed. Within twenty-four hours the blood clot dissipated.

Sometimes I would go through difficult financial situations, and she would stand fast, reminding me of some of the things Oral Roberts had been through.

Before Mary retired she told me my son-in-law should be our next administrator. When she said that to me, I thought it was the most impossible idea I had ever heard. She talked with him about it, and he laughed at her. He was an electrical engineer in Kansas City and happy in his work.

But two years later he and my daughter joined us in Denver, and he became our administrator. Mary saw my son-in-law was a problem-solver, and I have to say she was absolutely right.

Even though Mary and her husband retired to Tulsa, we still talk several times a month. We share prayer requests, and when I'm in Tulsa, we always have a meal together.

Only God could have given me a friend like Mary Smith. She stuck with me through hard times, good times, times when I was weak, when I was strong, times when I was in God's will, and times when I wasn't—and she still had confidence that I would come through. I will always be grateful to God and to her.

The day Mary came to stand by me, Mary chose to stick by my side through thick and thin, good and bad. And so she has.

I REMEMBER TIMES
WHEN YOU STOOD WITH ME . . .

❏ THROUGH HARD TIMES

❏ THROUGH GOOD TIMES

❏ THROUGH TIMES WHEN I WAS WEAK

❏ THROUGH TIMES WHEN I WAS STRONG,

❏ THROUGH TIMES WHEN I WAS IN
GOD'S WILL . . .

❏ AND TIMES WHEN I MISSED IT—

AND YOU STILL HAD CONFIDENCE
THAT I WOULD COME THROUGH.

MARILYN HICKEY

MARILYN IS A PASTOR'S WIFE, MOTHER, HOMEMAKER, AND THE FOUNDER OF MARILYN HICKEY MINISTRIES. THIS INTERNATIONAL ORGANIZATION HAS MINISTERED TO MILLIONS OF PEOPLE THROUGH PROJECTS, CONVENTIONS, COUNSELING SERVICES, A BIBLE COLLEGE, AND RADIO AND TELEVISION. MARRIED IN 1954, MARILYN AND HER HUSBAND, WALLACE, LIVE IN DENVER AND HAVE TWO CHILDREN.

Sisters and friends—Lisa, Andrea, and Joy Danielle

Lessons in togetherness

(Lisa, Andrea, and Joy Danielle)
as told to Jennifer Schott

e have a special bond of friendship because we're sisters. When we were growing up, we weren't allowed to watch much television so we were forced to find creative ways to spend our free time. One of our favorite activities was to play different albums such as Whitney Houston or Crystal Lewis and sing along. We would perform for each other. Since I was the oldest, I would try to arrange it so that I would get all the good songs. But I would let my younger sisters perform first. By the time my turn came around, they were fast asleep.

In 1990 our family moved to Nashville, and we entered talent shows, and soon began dancing for a number of contemporary Christian artists. While dancing at the 1991 Gospel Music Association's Dove Awards, we met d.c. talk and we began to tour together in 1993.

Talk about a learning experience! We didn't have everything that d.c. talk had. We didn't have a bus. We didn't have a road manager. We did have a 1977 Chevy van. And we slept in that, with Andrea and Joy Danielle on the pullout sofa and myself in the passenger seat. You can imagine my crankiness after these fabulous nights of sleep.

Our friendship was strained to the point of breaking. We would get on each other's nerves, and then we would start picking on each other. When you're sisters, you really know what to say to get things going.

Our tour chaplain, Michael Guido, told us, "You all need to learn how to be sisters in Christ."

It's easy to take each other for granted when you're sisters, but Michael pointed out to us that we wouldn't treat sisters in the Lord the way we were treating each other. So we learned God has called us to be slow to wrath, slow to speak, quick to listen, and to walk in love with each other.

As sisters, we have built-in accountability. It's possible for anyone to become prideful, but as sisters, you can take turns being the strong one, the one who calls on the others to get themselves in focus with reality.

Accountability came to the fore when Joy Danielle was going through her short-skirt phase and struggling with dating people who weren't Christians. It was hard for her because she was an example for others, but at the same time, she was going through the same things any other fifteen year old is trying to figure out.

Our manager at the time, Kathy Phillips, shared with us a scripture in James, which says teachers are called to higher levels. We're held even more accountable because we're telling people about God. That was a lesson that all of us had to learn.

I had to let them hold me accountable for the music I listened to. I would never encourage teenagers to listen to some of the stuff I did. But I thought I was above it because I didn't "really pay attention" to the words. Then I realized that was the same excuse our audience gives.

You make a lot of sacrifices to be in a group. You have a lot of things *you* want to do, but there's never any time for you, your dreams, or your plans. But as sisters, friends, and musicians, there has to be space to be individuals—we've learned together.

out of eden

Lisa, Andrea, and Joy Danielle Kimmey were born into a creative family. Their mother was a classical pianist and their father a writer. The girls began their singing careers as the opening act for their mother's concerts. Their albums include *More Than You Know* and *Lovin' the Day*. They have been nominated for a Dove Award as well as the Nashville Music Awards.

my sister, my friend

 C3

Sisters have a special bond of friendship,
but it's easy to take each other for granted
as Lisa, Andrea, and Joy Danielle discovered.
And it's easy to start picking on each other.
I pledge to be . . .

swift to hear

slow to speak

and slow to wrath

so we can walk in love with each other.

Lucille McKinnon has been a friend of encouragement
to Vonette Bright and her family.

Vonette Bright

from bows to butter roses

Lucille McKinnon is one of the most creative, godly, and sensitive people I know. She is constantly thinking of ideas to present the gospel more effectively, particularly to children. I was a young, new bride when I met Lucille, a California congressman's wife. She and her husband had just returned to California from Washington, D.C., at the end of her husband's term of office. Seeking a speaker for their church, she had asked a mutual friend, Alice McIntire, if my husband and I might be available. We took the engagement.

When we met, Lucille and I felt an immediate rapport. She mentioned she wanted to meet Mrs. Louis Evans, Sr., our pastor's wife and a mentor to me, so I arranged a meeting at the Beverly Wilshire Hotel. We had time before the meeting to stop at the wholesale florist supply store on the east side of downtown Los Angeles, to which, as a newcomer to L.A., I had never been. So many beautiful ideas were presented for table arrangements and package wrapping, along with candles and ribbons of every color and width imaginable. My eyes were saucers the entire time. Lucille was buying Christmas supplies, and I kept an eye on what she chose to purchase; I was learning from my creative new friend.

That day Lucille presented me with a spectacularly wrapped gift, topped with a crisp bow. She mentioned she had done the bow herself, and she would teach me how to tie a package bow. I was an eager learner and have become the "major bow tier" at any event.

The next year my husband and I combined households with Henrietta Mears, director of Christian Education at Hollywood Presbyterian Church. Illness had forced her to take a several-month sabbatical. During that time, I encouraged her to teach a Bible class of women who lived close by. I would see the house was ready; prepare the juice, rolls, and coffee; and host the event. Lucille attended the class, and she did lots of spiritual growing during that time. God has gifted her with biblical insight, which she still shares with me often.

Our two sons were small, and Lucille took a real interest in them. She readily shared her child-rearing insights and had such clever ideas for activities and children's gifts. She realized my schedule was full, and so she would send care packages to the boys like sugar ice cream cones covered with pink crepe paper so they looked like strawberry cones. Underneath the make-believe ice cream, she placed a dollar bill or a Baskin-Robbins gift certificate.

One year, when the boys were about six and ten years old, she sent a do-it-yourself Easter kit. She provided examples of the steps to take for a family activity using empty eggshells. The shells had an opening on the side, then were dipped into melted paraffin and set to harden. Paper grass was added to form a nest. A miniature chick or rabbit was placed in the nest with a scripture verse printed on a tiny scroll prominently on or in the egg. This "egg fixing" became a tradition in our home.

When Zac, our eldest son, graduated from high school, she sent a college survival kit that included a modern translation of the Bible, *Webster's Collegiate Dictionary*, a thermos, a mug, hot chocolate mix, and packets of tea and coffee. As far as I know, Zac still uses some of these items.

My hobby is hospitality. I make an effort to glorify Christ in entertaining. From Lucille I learned to make butter roses for a special touch in entertaining and to put several geraniums together with a rubber band to make them look like one fabulous blossom. I benefited from so many of her ideas and her encouragement to express myself creatively.

She also collected quotes I could use in my public speaking. One I have often used is from an educational consultant for General Motors. He said, "Every individual, no matter in what remote part of the world he may live, influences at least 160 people in his lifetime." In speaking, I ask the question, "How are you influencing those 160 people?"

Lucille is always in the center of my rooting section, praying for me, encouraging me, believing in me, and helping me when she can. She's taught me about bows, butter roses, Easter eggs, and pithy quotes. But even more, I've learned from her about what it means to be a kind, generous friend. When I phone her, she responds as if I'm the most important person in her life. I know she has so many friends, travels the world, spends a lot of time in prayer, and volunteers when she can. A "friend of encouragement" describes her well. I pray the Lord will keep her around many more years. I need her for a long time to come.

vonette bright

with her husband, dr. bill bright, vonette founded campus crusade for christ international. a member of the original Lausanne committee for evangelization, vonette also served as chair of the intercession working group from 1981 to 1990. in 1988, as chair of the national day of prayer task force, vonette introduced legislation to make the first thursday in may of each year the national day of prayer. the brights live in orlando, florida. they are the parents of two sons, and the grandparents of four children.

KAREN MAINS

a polite but distant smile

the voice on the phone was Miriam's. It sounded slightly constricted, as if she was struggling to control nervousness.

"I would like to talk to you," she said. "Perhaps you've noticed the distance in our relationship. There is a flaw in me, something out of my past that made me vulnerable in our friendship. I would like to talk about this soon—if you want to, and have the time."

Noticed the distance in our relationship? Well, of course I had. Once, Miriam and I had been new and eager friends. We had met in church, where we quickly discovered areas of mutual interest. We enjoyed each other's minds and conversed intensely about the effect of spirituality on emotional and mental health.

Perhaps it all started too fast. Maybe we jumped into intimacy, bypassing the normal route of acquaintanceship. At any rate, while doing committee work together something happened. There was no overt breach, no harsh word, no apparent disagreement; but suddenly a growing friendship aborted. Without discussion, Miriam and I slipped into that all-too-familiar Christian state of polite but distant smiles in the church lobby.

At first, I was wary of her attempt at reconciliation. I remembered times when others had come to me, blurting out what I had done wrong and pronouncing forgiveness before asking my perception of the problem. "There now," they would say on the way out, "I'm so glad we had this little talk. I feel infinitely better."

Usually, I felt infinitely worse.

When Miriam called after more than a year of polite coolness, I was intrigued. She wanted to discuss a flaw from her past. How could I refuse so gentle an offer of peace?

Still, I wondered how we would end our time together. Would the appointment merely air her griefs and leave me feeling the weight of my wrongs? Something in that approach prevented true reconciliation. It kept me and my forgiver at a polite distance.

The day finally came. Miriam sat in my living room, her soft brown hair curling around her face. The old-fashioned clock ticked off the seconds in the quiet.

My friend cleared her throat to begin, and I braced myself for the difficulties ahead. *No matter the approach,* I told myself, *this effort is taking great courage on Miriam's part. Remember she is of great value, not only to you but also to God. Be gentle and loving, whatever she says. Love is the rule. Listen well so you can learn truth about yourself. There is truth in every criticism.*

But to my amazement, there was no finger-pointing, no blame cast. Miriam spoke of problems from her past, of growing up feeling unloved. This deprivation had created a hole in her person, she said, and she sometimes still stumbled into it. During our work on the committee, my take-charge personality had suddenly made her feel incompetent.

"I just dried up and quietly blew away," she said. But her explanation carried no hint of accusation.

"I would have come to you sooner," she continued, "but it has taken me this long to figure it out, why it happened, and what wound in myself left me so vulnerable."

Miriam didn't pronounce forgiveness upon me; she asked me to

forgive her! She wasn't asking me to change, but only to understand. What she was doing was far riskier than the quick reconciliation attempts I had seen before. She was taking responsibility for
her own reactions, claiming her role in the breach between us, and
leaving the results to the Holy Spirit.

The defenses that I had so carefully erected to prevent damage
to myself were unnecessary. With all my sympathies aroused for my
friend's pain, I had the freedom to examine how I might have contributed to the problem. It takes two people to make a friendship,
I reminded myself, and two people to break one. What had I unin-
tentionally done wrong? How could I keep from doing it again?
What steps should I take to restore the relationship?

Miriam and I are still in the process of reconstruction. We met
regularly for several months to resume our interrupted communication. Now we touch base every so often and catch up in church.
Recently, she informed me that in her mind we hadn't made as
much progress in our relationship as I thought we had.

"I want a friendship with you on whatever level you would
like," I replied. "But if you want to go deeper, you'll have to teach
me what you mean. Sometimes I don't know exactly what you
expect."

Out of such honesty is true friendship formed. Miriam and I are
learning a fuller meaning of reconciliation—the willingness to
enter into pain together, the courage to explore truth about ourselves. A devotional writer once stated:

> As long as we are on earth, the love that unites us will bring us
> suffering by our very contact with one another, because this love is
> the resetting of a Body of broken bones. Even saints cannot live
> with saints on this earth without some anguish, without some pain
> at the differences that come between them.
>
> There are two things which men can do about the pain of dis-
> union with other men. They can love or they can hate. Hatred

recoils from the sacrifice and the sorrow that are the price of this resetting of bones. It refuses the pain of reunion.

Miriam has taught me what I suspected all along. Reconciliation is not simple; it is a matter of setting broken bones. There is agony in the dislocation, agony in the resetting. And few of us love enough to take on the godly humility that says: "This is where I have broken the Body. This is where I am frail within. What can I do to make it right?"

Only in this vulnerability is there true reconciliation.

karen mains

karen is an award-winning author and communicator and is actively involved in radio and television broadcasting. she served on the board of intervarsity christian fellowship for eight years and was elected the first woman chairperson. she is co-executive director with her husband, david, of the chapel ministries, which produces a daily half-hour national television show, *you need to know.* she is the author of twenty some books, including *open heart, open home* and *comforting one another.*

LYNN HALLIMORE

WHERE TWO ARE GATHERED

he answer began at a church banquet. While our husbands excused themselves to search for the punch bowl, the four wives at the table began discussing a recent book on protecting marriages.

Then Kristine said, "You know what we should do? Let's get together and pray for our husbands and families."

I felt my heart beat faster. For the past three weeks, ever since moving into this community, I had been asking God for a prayer partner. Our move had heightened my awareness of the spiritual needs in my family and neighborhood, but I knew I couldn't carry the prayer load myself.

Kristine's green eyes glowed with understanding as I told her my story. "It began the morning I read Mark 2:1–12," I said. "I felt just like the men who carried their lame friend to Jesus. The paralytic must have been a large man. It took four friends, one for each corner, straining in unison.

"Likewise, I feel this great burden to bring my family and community before the Lord in prayer. But I need help carrying the stretcher. So I began praying for a unique prayer partner, one who got excited about loaded stretchers!"

Kristine is mom to a two year old. I have a teenager and a ten year old. Kristine has a professional career background. I'm a homemaker. She loves city life. I breathe easier on the fringe of the suburbs, where the sidewalk ends. But God planted the same desire in our hearts.

After Kristine and I agreed to be prayer partners, we had to arrange a time and place to pray. "How about Friday mornings, my house?" I asked, after learning she lived only a mile away.

"Good," Kristine answered. "I'll drop Emily at the sitter's, then swing over at 10:00 A.M."

Though we invited other women to join us, not everyone was excited about carrying stretchers for an hour a week. The reasons sounded a lot like ones I had used myself: "My schedule's too full." "I can't arrange child care." "I don't pray aloud." "I find group prayer intimidating." "An hour!?"

At our first meeting, we developed a structure for praying. Feeling comfortable in conversational prayer, we chose that as our format— each taking turns praying in paragraphs. We began with praise, thanksgiving, and confession to fortify us and prepare us to be stretcher-bearers. We asked that our will would be aligned to God's.

Then, rather than discussing our prayer requests, we simply brought them directly to God. This ensured that we prayed more than we visited.

At first, we knew little about each other. We even struggled to remember the names of the other's children. Yet, we both felt comfortable being open and vulnerable. Our responses before God ranged from tears to laughter.

If one drew a mental blank while praying, the other filled in. Kristine began, "Lord, we lift up Loren and Starla's little one . . . Lynn, what's her name?"

"Shelby," I replied.

"That's her, Lord—Shelby, the one who fell. We ask for healing for Shelby."

Because of our common bond in Christ and the unity of our

purpose, our first meeting went smoothly. Yet like the men who carried the lame man, we would face obstacles, both physical and spiritual.

Friday morning the phone sat silent—until we began praying. The grandmother clock chimed its longest repertoire. The dog yapped at anything. My stomach roared, even though I'd eaten an hour earlier. I continued praying louder and louder.

Kristine broke into giggles. I soon followed. "What do you think God's expression looks like now?" she asked.

"I think He's rolling His eyes, shaking His head, and laughing with us."

In the weeks that followed, we met other obstacles. Kristine juggled child care. Vacations interrupted our usual meeting time. Her little one woke up ill. One morning I found my dog frothing at the mouth. "Kristine, I have to take the dog into the vet this morning. I'm sorry. Can you believe this?"

"Lynn, Satan wants to keep us from praying. But we'll find a way. Keep me posted. I'll rearrange my child care."

I thanked God for Kristine's commitment. Though at first I had envisioned four women praying together, God knew what He was doing. Two schedules were easier to rearrange than four.

Some mornings, my feelings did not match my initial enthusiasm to pray. But I knew that faith and obedience could push past every obstacle. So I exercised reluctant self-discipline and prayed anyway. Once we entered God's presence, I often would marvel inwardly, *And to think, I almost did not come!*

Each Friday morning, Kristine and I found ourselves echoing that amazement and joy as we marked answered prayers in our journals.

The first discovery involved finding renewed energy and spiritual refreshment when we had grown tired of dragging our loaded stretchers alone.

Although praying for her father-in-law's salvation had grown stale for Kristine over the years, I could pray with fresh enthusiasm.

Likewise, she prayed about house plans that my husband and I had given up discussing. The advantage of a new perspective helps bolster the other's faith.

Often during this time, God combined Kristine's words with His promptings to guide and instruct me. For instance, I was concerned about our ten-year-old son, Jericho. The move had been hardest on him because he had to change schools. Then a classmate, along with some older students, ridiculed and humiliated the "new kid" during the school bus ride home.

A brief meeting with his teacher informed me of the challenges Jericho faced. "Out of fifteen years as a teacher, this has been my toughest class. Normally, a teacher expects one troublemaker per class; this one has eight."

Jericho had one more month of school left. I prayed for his protection, his discernment, his spirit's healing, and his confidence.

Then Kristine's soft voice began, "Lord, work in the hearts of the children who acted so cruelly. They need Your love in their lives. Help Jericho to be a shining light for You on dark days."

I had prayed as a protective parent. Kristine prayed with a larger perspective. Her words helped me recognize the opportunity for doing good, for building character, and for learning to overcome difficulty by relying on God.

Another time, my freshman daughter informed me, "Mom, you know that girl in my health class who has her nose, ears, eyebrows, lip, and navel pierced? Well, today she told this guy in class she was being suspended for selling drugs. She said, 'I haven't come to this class once without being high on something!'"

My heart turned to lead. But when I laid my teenager and her classmate on the stretcher, the heaviness lifted as Kristine and I prayed in unison.

Because we prayed for those in our immediate circle of influence, we saw God's answers up close and personal. After we prayed, Kristine's husband, Peter, was able to visit his ailing father in Ecuador.

We also prayed that Jericho's school would remove a book with profanity and vulgarity from the required reading list. After my husband, John, and I met with the review committee, they agreed to request its removal.

We prayed for the neighborhood Bible study that John began in our home. What an encouragement when the group made a commitment to reach our community for Jesus—starting with a block party.

The other day, Kristine looked up at my grandmother clock and asked, "Lynn, is that clock right?" It seemed unbelievable that we had prayed for an hour and a half! Our visit with God felt so warm and bracing, we found ourselves reluctant to stop.

Week by week, load by load, one stretcher at a time, we set the needy before Jesus. Each encounter leaves us anticipating the next. The memory of our time with God and each other draws us past every obstacle to the feet of the One who bids us, "Come."

LYNN HALLIMORE

LYNN HALLIMORE, a freelance writer, has articles published in numerous Christian periodicals and adult Bible studies. She serves on her church's drama team, mentoring program, and women's ministries board. She enjoys teaching and speaking on topics of family, discipleship, and prayer. Lynn has worked in the medical field for twenty years. Her current position working with a cardiologist gives her an evergrowing love for senior citizens. Lynn and her husband, John, have two teenage children, Jessica and Jericho. Their family attends Lakeside Church in Folsom, California. This article originally appeared in *Moody Monthly* magazine.

Part two

✦ moments of DIVERSITY ✦

My friend Toni Caldwell with her husband, Kim,
and their daughters, Ashley and Alex

teRRy Meeuwsen

JUSt as we aRe

he sun was shining, and I was humming happy tunes as I drove down the road. Our family was back in Milwaukee for our first visit since moving to Virginia Beach. And I was going to spend the day with my friend Toni Caldwell, whom I hadn't seen since we had left. I had anticipated this day for a long time.

Since our daughters had been best friends for several years, Toni and I decided to rendezvous at Discovery Zone, where the girls could play and we could visit. Toni, as pretty as ever, was just getting out of her car when I pulled into the parking lot.

Her daughter, Ashley, and my Tory went skipping and laughing ahead of us, happy to be together again. Ashley was nine and an only child. Tory was seven and had three brothers.

I hugged Toni. For a moment it seemed we still lived a short distance from each other and were just getting together for one of our lunches. After we settled the girls, we headed for the food area to place our order. "My treat; how about pizza and sodas?" I asked.

"That's fine for Ashley. I'll have an apple and some milk."

I looked at her in disbelief. "An apple and some milk? Don't you feel good?"

Toni looked a little flustered and stammered a bit. "No, I'm fine. I-I just . . ."

I can't tell you how I knew, but my eyes grew wide in amazement. "Toni, are you pregnant?"

She didn't have to say a word; the sparkle in her eyes said it all. Soon we were laughing, crying, and hugging each other. The young clerk behind the cash register had witnessed all this and offered her congratulations as she rang up our order.

This was indeed a moment to rejoice. For years Toni and her husband, Kim, had hoped to no avail for a brother or sister for Ashley. Toni was ecstatic. I couldn't stop crying. Needless to say, this little miracle, only a few weeks along, dominated our conversation that day.

Several months later, I received a call from Toni. After saying hello she began to cry softly. My heart sank. My first thought was a miscarriage. She shared haltingly that some preliminary tests had been taken to monitor the baby's well-being. The doctor had just called to say the tests indicated Toni was carrying a Down's syndrome baby. Toni and Kim were devastated. She and I talked, cried, and prayed.

At the end of our conversation, I said, "Toni, this is easy for me to say because this isn't my pregnancy, my life, or my baby, but I know several families with Down's children, and they are so special. In fact, in every one of those families, the parents tell me that having the Down's child has been a blessing that has enriched their family. While this isn't the route you would have chosen for yourself, God has a plan, and we both know He doesn't make mistakes.

"And Toni, I don't know of a more wonderful home or family that God could entrust a special needs child to than yours. You and Kim are wonderful parents, and Ashley will love this baby no matter what. This is a shock, but God will equip you with whatever you need to work this out. I just know it." But even as I spoke, I felt their anguish and loss in my own heart.

Toni called a couple of days later, and I was amazed at how she and Kim had surrendered their plans, hopes, and dreams to the Lord. They were staunchly defending the life and rights of this child to any imagined foe. I smiled as I listened to Toni. This little family was allowing God to enlarge their hearts and lives with the challenge set before them. As I watched from the sidelines, my own faith was stirred and enriched.

On April 10, 1994, Alexandra Grace Caldwell was born without a trace of Down's syndrome! How we rejoiced! But how blessed I had been by my friend's willingness to accept God's plan with courage and faith.

Oh, one other aspect of our friendship you might be interested to know: Toni's family is black, and my family is . . . well, Heinz 57. Andy, Drew, Tory, and I are white. J. P. is Korean, and Tyler is biracial. Toni and I have often talked about the issue of race and how it affects all of us.

I have heard it said God is color-blind. I think the opposite is true. God loves uniqueness and diversity. I don't think He intended for us to compare ourselves to each other. I think He wants us to celebrate the beauty and the uniqueness of each of us.

This little poem hangs in our family room:

> *If all of us kids were just black or white*
> *then maybe everything would be all right.*
> *But there's Carlo's black hair,*
> *so straight and so fine, and Becky's red curls,*
> *so different from mine.*
> *And Angela's dark skin*
> *is so pretty, it seems,*
> *while Julie's gold locks are a thing made of dreams.*
> *Chuckie's eyes slant*
> *in a way that's just so . . .*
> *I like when he laughs*

and his face seems to glow.
So just when I think the the world would be right
If we were all black, or maybe all white
I stop and wonder if we're not better by far
For loving our differences, just as they are.

Copyright © 1987 Claudia Rohling

Friendship knows no barrier of race, position, creed, age, or color. In the following stories women express how they have found meaningful relationships with those who differ from them socially, culturally, religiously, or ethnically. These sagas remind us that friendship is too creative and too genuine to respect those kinds of boundaries.

◆   ◆   ◆

"A friend is a present you give yourself."
—Robert Louis Stevenson

Pam Mellskog

BEYOND THE BLUE

ersonally, I don't think blue hair does much for her looks, but my friend Cole dyes her tangled coif that color because she likes it. Some may say Cole's blue hair only makes a red flag of her insecurities, her style begs for reaction. And, in-as-much as a fashion statement can ask a question, that may be true. At age seventeen, Cole wants to know who sees her and who sees blue.

Tonight, though, there's more than just blue to behold. She's wearing a sequined, lemon-colored chiffon dress with black fishnet gloves and matching stockings. Copper, brass, and studded leather bracelets wind up her forearms like charmed snakes on a modern Cleopatra. Yet, as we devour a platterful of pizza in Uptown, the most trendy, tolerant part of Minneapolis, no one notices this but me. Only I hear the many safety pins and mini-hoops faintly clinking from her ear lobes, and only I watch the wire dream-catcher earring she made this afternoon sway with the erratic motion of our conversation. In this part of the city, anything goes. Uptown passes no judgment on Cole.

But Cole doesn't live in Uptown. She lives in Prior Lake, a farflung conservative suburb where people judge differences more harshly. There, some think she's an "evil, bad kid." Others simply

+ 57

dub her crowd the "dirt balls." That's the impression her track coach got at the start of Cole's first season on the team. When the teenager lettered in the sport, however, he presented an apology along with the honor. He admitted he had judged Cole on her appearance and, in the end, had underestimated her.

Interestingly, adults aren't the only ones who judge and label. At the state fair last summer, some similarly clad teenagers sniffing around for marijuana approached Cole. (To them, she looked like she'd be in the know.)

Being mistakenly identified as "that type of kid" by both track coaches and peers bothers Cole. Yet, she is intentional about her alternative style and uses the controversy it raises to challenge stereotypes. Part of her unique niche as a Christian, she says, is showing that one doesn't have to look a certain way to achieve high standards or to have a good attitude.

"I want people to say, 'Yeah, that's Cole. She's a little different, a little weird, but she has her head on straight.' I feel God wants me to show others that He can shine through anybody who looks any way." Cole explains. "I could be an ordinary-looking student. But if I change just one simple thing—my appearance—and it changes somebody's mind, makes them less judgmental, then I'd rather do that. I think that can glorify God too."

I had first met Cole last summer on a church-sponsored back-packing trip to Colorado. She was a camper, and I was a counselor nearly twice her age. One day we broke off from the group to hike a steeper climb. Our maiden voyage serpentined through the timber and beyond the July snowline to the foot of a tumbling water-fall. After carefully scaling the slick black shale alongside it, we discovered the reward for our efforts—a chilly, still lake eleven thousand feet above sea level.

But I had found more reason to rejoice in God's unique creation than just the gorgeous scenery; my hiking companion embodied the wonders of God's broad creative vision. Huffing and puffing, we had talked most of the way up, and I had discovered in this "dirt ball" a young woman who took on the mountains with a "Let's go!" attitude. I had also learned that, in addition to running track, she played volleyball and liked to write morality essays and poetry.

In spite of her determination to look beneath the surface, Cole still misses the mark. Once, for example, she avoided a schoolmate because the girl struck her as an arrogant, high-society high schooler, someone she could never befriend. Now, Cole describes her as a sweetheart and can't imagine how she ever judged this shy one with such conviction. "If I'm going to be different, I should be open-minded about everybody else."

It's getting late, and the pizza is almost gone. Before we call it a night, however, I ask about the dark cross tattooed on Cole's left shoulder underneath the yellow dress strap. She says she designed it to raise questions with peers and to show them that Christians come in many packages.

The conversation moves on to James 2, the passage in which two men come to a meeting, one in fine clothes and the other in rags. The Bible warns us not to judge, not to show the rich man a better seat while sending the poor man to sit on the floor. If we do so, the writer says, "have you not discriminated among yourselves and become judges with evil thoughts" (v. 4, NIV)?

Cole identifies with the poor man. Like him, she could command more instant respect if she made herself look more acceptable to mainstream society. But the point of our faith, she and I agree, is essence over form. Again and again, Jesus made this clear through His teachings, the heart is the sole measure of a person.

And Cole, a teenage Christian with a flair for being different, takes that charge seriously. By putting herself in jeopardy of being judged like the poor man, she hopes to see life and faith from a radically different perspective.

While paying the bill, I mused that young Cole carries at least one tongue of flame from the torch of Mother Teresa, who had died in Calcutta just two weeks earlier. And I remember the elderly woman said she saw good in every face. Abject poverty and sickness never fooled her.

What is blue hair to hinder us?

pam meLLskog
pam is a freelance writer
who lives in minnesota. this
article originally appeared
in *virtue magazine*.

♦ ♦ ♦

"When you're with someone you trust in,
never needing to pretend,
Someone who helps you know yourself,
you know you're with a friend."
—Amanda Bradley

ɴot too faʀ fʀom Heʀe

n early 1985 I served as a telephone counselor for *The 700 Club* telethon. I was to take pledges from supporters and to pray with people calling in to ask about salvation or to express special needs.

One of the callers was Susan, a seventeen-year-old prostitute, drug addict, and alcoholic—who had just found out she was pregnant! It was the last straw, she said. What would she do with a baby? She confided she couldn't kill a baby by having an abortion but she could kill herself. Can you imagine my horror?

This was my first night to be a counselor of any type, and I got *this* call! I started to flip frantically through my counselor's handbook, but I soon realized it wasn't going to help. As Susan continued to talk, I silently prayed for the Lord's guidance in speaking to this desperate young woman.

That night Susan accepted Jesus as her Savior. I gave her my telephone number, and she gave me hers so we could stay in contact.

Susan and I had many heart-to-heart conversations over the next ten years. We talked about God loving her no matter what. We discussed the consequences of her actions before becoming a Christian. We cried when she miscarried her baby. She had no close family relationships so she spent two Christmas holidays with my family. In short, I tried to be there for her.

Susan brought a new dimension into my life. I had never known anyone who had been a prostitute or a drug addict. Through my relationship with this precious girl, I found out my own sins were no less sinful than hers; they were just better hidden.

As time went on, the time between phone calls grew. Weeks stretched into months. I knew I should call to see how she was doing, but I kept putting it off.

Then two years ago, on my birthday, the phone rang. "Kim," my father said, and I knew by the tone of his voice that something was wrong. "We just received a call from a friend of Susan's. She said Susan had been sick and hospitalized for the past two weeks. I hesitated to call you on your birthday, but I thought you would want to know . . . Susan died today."

My heart sank. Why hadn't I stayed in touch with her? My consolation was, of course, knowing that Susan was no longer sick or lonely. She isn't too far from here; she's singing with the angels in heaven.

Susan taught me many things over the course of our ten-year friendship. Her final lesson, though, was perhaps the most important: Don't put off doing something you feel led to do. We always think we can do a good deed, say a kind word, or attend to a special need *tomorrow*. Sometimes there is no tomorrow, only today.

✦　✦　✦

"Friends are people with whom you share
your time and also your heart."
—Unknown

KIM BOYCE

IN 1984 KIM WAS MISS FLORIDA AND WAS NAMED A SEMI-FINALIST IN THE MISS AMERICA PAGEANT. AFTER MOVING TO NASHVILLE TO PURSUE A CAREER IN CONTEMPORARY CHRISTIAN MUSIC, SHE PRODUCED SEVEN ALBUMS AND TWO VIDEOS AND RECEIVED TWO DOVE NOMINATIONS. SHE HAS WRITTEN FOUR BOOKS INCLUDING HER MOST RECENT, *DREAMS I'M DREAMIN'*. KIM AND HER HUSBAND, GARY KOREIBA, HAVE TWO YOUNG SONS. THIS ARTICLE WAS TAKEN FROM *DREAMS I'M DREAMIN'*. COPYRIGHT © 1997 BY KIM BOYCE. PUBLISHED BY SERVANT PUBLICATIONS, BOX 8617, ANN ARBOR, MI, 48107. USED WITH PERMISSION.

Chonda Pierce and Doris, opposites but best of friends, enjoy their zany moments together.

the Language of Girlfriends

 ello?" *I answered the phone.*

"Is this a hag-head trip?" Doris, my best friend, asked.

"No. We have to be ready when we get there," I explained.

"Oh, that's a corn-killer. What dog-head planned our schedule like that?"

"It was the only flight available."

"Oh, brother, are we on one of those doohickeys?"

"I'm afraid so, but I do think the plane has a bathroom on it."

"I'll be swanee. I'm worn out. I'll just put my face on when I get there."

The language of girlfriends! I have no idea what a doohickey is, but when Doris calls something a doohickey, I know *exactly* what she's talking about. Sometimes that scares me. But most of the time I revel that we connect with each other so well. Not only do we borrow one another's clothes, make-up, and other doohickeys, but we also have reached the point we understand each other's language.

Because of my job, I travel a lot; I'm a comedian. Fortunately, I get to travel with an incredible piano player who just happens to be my girlfriend Doris. We've been doing this for years now.

I remember once Doris and I had driven all day to Birmingham, Alabama. When we pulled into the parking lot of our hotel, she looked at me and said, "It's a shame we didn't drive. We could have gone to that mall back there when we're done." I just stared at her across the dashboard. "Doris, what do you think this is?" I slapped vinyl.

She stared for a moment. Then her eyes slowly cleared, and the fog lifted away. "Oh, that's right. We're in the van!" (We usually fly everywhere. That's why Doris is more accustomed to the interior of a 747 than a Mercury Villager.)

I just about fell out of the plane—I mean, van.

She can certainly make me laugh!

And Doris has a contagious laugh. First her face puckers up (that's not so bad); then she makes a snorting sound like something from deep in the forest (and that's not so bad either). But then she pulls back her left hand and slaps whatever or whoever is within arm's length. (Never sit near Doris at a funny movie, especially if you don't have comprehensive medical coverage.)

In most ways, Doris and I are opposites. (On some occasions I have been known to snort, but she's much louder than I am.) We have different tastes in clothes and music; I'm tall, she's short; I'm blonde, she's brunette; I am my brother's sister, and she is my brother's wife. But for all our differences, we seem stuck together. But isn't that the way it is with girlfriends?

Ruth and Naomi were in-laws too, and like us, opposites. (Of course, there is no mention of a mall in the Bible so I'm not sure how they stood on the clothes issue.) Ruth was a Gentile, Naomi a Hebrew. Ruth was young, Naomi was older. Naomi was wise in Scripture, Ruth was willing to sit at her feet and learn. Tragedy and survival brought them together in a relationship bound with love, trust, loyalty, and commitment. Both had watched their husbands die. Both were left alone. But their remarkable friendship (because they were also girlfriends) withstood their diversity. The devotion they expressed to each other provides an incredible role model for any relationship.

The *Woman's Study Bible* lists these attributes of a friendship:

♦ Gratitude on the part of one awakens loyalty in the heart of the other.

♦ Selflessness on the part of one demands unselfishness from the other.

♦ Bitterness in one gives opportunity for creativity in the other.

♦ Interest from one is rewarded by responsible communication from the other.

♦ Counsel from one bears fruit as accepted and honored by the other.

Ruth and Naomi, like all girlfriends, expressed those qualities in their relationship.

At times Doris and I lean on one another for much more than a recipe for lemon icebox pie (my husband's favorite). Sometimes, when we can't even express our pain, the language of a girlfriend goes beyond what can be uttered. After all, the lexicon for girlfriends isn't filled entirely with words. Through its bulk of pages you will also see snorts, slaps, hugs, and tears. In this language there are even moments of no language, just silence. This silence is filled with understanding and strength. (This one is tough for me, but Doris is teaching me well.)

The language also includes a look, a touch, a nod of the head, a presence that says "Go ahead and fall. I'll catch you. Even if I'm way across the room, I'll run and catch you like that mom on the television commercial who catches the falling cake before it can stain her carpet."

When my older sister died in a car accident, Doris wept with me. Several months later, when my little sister died of leukemia, Doris wept with me again. Several years later, when Doris' mother died, I drove her two sons to the mall and helped them pick out some clothes to wear to the funeral. Then I hurried back—so I could weep with Doris.

Doris called me a few days ago. "I'm having a hissie-fit."

"I know, but they'll be gone in a few more weeks."

"This is terrible. I hope I'll be retired and in Florida the next time they get here."

"Doris, you're so old you'll probably view them from Heaven the next time they come for a visit."

"They just cling to you and make obnoxious noises. You can't even get to the car without them swarming all over you."

Swarming? "Whoa, wait a minute! Are we talking about the same thing?"

"I'm talking about these stinkin' cicadas. What are you talking about?"

"I thought you were talking about your in-laws!"

I guess even Doris and I can get a little confused with the language of girlfriends.

chonda pierce

chonda is a comedian, speaker, author, and recording artist. she speaks at aspiring women and women of faith conferences and currently is touring "havin' a girls' nite out!" with her girlfriend, doris.

the give-and-take of
our friendship

ↄ3

Like ruth and naomi, like chonda and
doris, we are also very different, but you
have expressed your friendship to me in
some very remarkable ways . . .

❏ gratitude on your part awakens loyalty
in mine

❏ selflessness on your part demands
unselfishness from me

❏ bitterness in one of our hearts gives the
other opportunity for creativity

❏ interest from you inspires responsible
communication from me

❏ counsel from you bears fruit as accepted
and honored by me

the Greeks have stolen my heart

pposites attract, so they say. And I think they're right. For more than twenty-five years I have been close friends with a Greek family who lives in Athens. From all outward experience, we have little in common. We don't think in the same language, live in the same country, share the same culture, or embrace the same political values. Perhaps most significantly, we do not have the same philosophy of life. Nevertheless, our friendship has grown and blossomed. That's because we've found common ground in matters of the heart. We love each other.

The first Stylianidou family member I met was Sophia. Through her I met her older sister, Klea; Klea's husband, Achilles; and their daughter, Madelene. Sophia's parents, Panagiotis and Maria, became my friends as well. I was a tourist in Greece when I met them and have since returned eight times to be their houseguest.

Because of the stark differences between us, the distance in miles, and the obvious work it took to keep this friendship alive, there were numerous times I could have given up. But I can honestly say that thought never crossed my mind. I can't imagine my life without my Greek friends in it. In fact, the challenge of keeping up-to-date has been a great part of the joy.

Through the years, we have wept, laughed, mourned, and danced together. Numerous friends of mine have met Sophia when they have visited Athens. With great intensity and enthusiasm we have maintained a system of letter writing and gift giving that has bonded us even more. But the most important thing we have enjoyed together is the conversation: face-to-face, by telephone, or in those letters. We've said it all!

During my most recent visit, Klea and I had one of our usual delightful conversations. She was wearing a rather large ring I was admiring, which became translucent when held up to the light. Etched into it was the Greek god, Jupiter. The exchange went something like this:

K: "Lusaki, do you know Jupiter?"

L: "You mean the Greek god, Jupiter?"

K: "Yes."

L: "Well, yes, somewhat . . . but what about him?"

K: "He is the god who changed himself into other forms to do something he wanted to do. On this ring he has changed himself into rain . . . can you see it?" (She held it up to the light.)

L: "Oh, yes, I see it . . . but why did he become rain?"

K: "Because he wanted to make love with Danae."

L: "Danae? Who is Danae?"

K: (With a flick of her wrist and a thoughtful look) "Oh, I don't know . . . some Greek godness."

I howled. Everything so serious and accurate till the end of the story; then, as though she tired of her own storytelling, "Oh, I don't know . . . some Greek godness." I *cracked up!*

On that same trip, Klea and I had several conversations about the Lord. In fact, I walked through her door one day and the first thing she said was, "Lusaki, tell me everything you know about

God." I couldn't tell her everything, but I had the opportunity to share the gospel. Little did I know that would be my last conversation with Klea. She died this year of breast cancer. Across the miles, Sophia and I have tried to comfort one another in our grief. This has been a profound loss.

One of my great concerns—something I see frequently in Christian circles—is the tendency to isolate ourselves from those who are different from us. We gravitate toward people who think like we think, agree with us on everything, believe like we do, even dress the same. In so doing we miss wonderful, God-given opportunities to expand our understanding of the world and the people in it.

Jesus prayed for us about this, specifically in John 17:15 and 18: "My prayer is not that you take them out of the world but that you protect them from the evil one . . . As you sent me into the world, I have sent them into the world" (NIV).

In this world, I wouldn't have wanted to miss the Stylianidou family . . . not one single member.

LUCI SWINDOLL

LUCI IS THE FORMER VICE-PRESIDENT OF PUBLIC RELATIONS FOR INSIGHT FOR LIVING AND THE AUTHOR OF NUMEROUS BOOKS, INCLUDING *Celebrating Life*. SHE IS A REGULAR SPEAKER AT THE WOMEN OF FAITH CONFERENCES. "THE GREEKS HAVE STOLEN MY HEART" BY LUCI SWINDOLL APPEARED IN THE BOOK *JOY BREAKS* BY PATSY CLAIRMONT, BARBARA JOHNSON, MARILYN MEBERG, AND LUCI SWINDOLL. COPYRIGHT © 1997 BY NEW LIFE CLINICS. USED BY PERMISSION OF ZONDERVAN PUBLISHING HOUSE.

Let's celebrate our diversity

℘

we are the same . . .

we are much alike in that we both . . .

_____

_____

_____

_____

but we are different . . .

we are different in that

I am _____ and you are _____

I like _____ and you like _____

I believe _____ while you believe _____

I enjoy wearing _____ while you wear _____

You are from _____ while I am from _____

I tend to be _____ while you tend to be _____

we are different
but bonded in love.

Madeline Manning Mims

◆ ◆ ◆

"Definition of a friend: Someone especially sent
by God to encourage you."
—Unknown

the odd couple

When an eleven-year-old girl, whose stature was that of a six year old, walked into the church's choir room to join the junior choir, she stunned us all with her bold personality. She was asked to give her name and to try out for the choir by singing something.

"My name is Gloria Lyons, and I'm eleven years old, even though you may not believe that. I can sing from low alto to high soprano so wherever you need me to sing, I'll be happy to oblige you."

At first, all of us choir members were silent. Then the altos and sopranos were calling for her to come to their section, as if they could outbid each other for this fascinating waif.

The choir director asked her if she knew any songs to sing.

"Sure! Do you know how to play 'His Eye Is on the Sparrow'?"

We all chuckled until she told the choir director what key to play it in and the style in which she wanted it played. What happened next is hard to describe. She opened her little mouth, and this huge, soulful voice came booming forth. When she finished, there wasn't a dry eye in the place, and she had shown us Jesus. My heart bonded with her from afar.

She was sent to our section, where the thirteen year olds were.

As she sat beside me, a shy teenager, she looked me square in the eye, and said, "Hi! What's your name? I'm Gloria."

Blushingly, I responded, "Hi, my name is Madeline."

From that day on, our lives became entwined with love and admiration for each other. She was everything I wanted to be: bold, outspoken, cheerful, and living life at its fullest. She never gave up, never broke down, never tried to break out. She just walked through staunch challenges, and even the valley of the shadow of death, fearing no evil, for she knew God was with her. I marveled at her strength and ability to laugh in the face of overwhelming circumstances.

You see, Gloria Lyons, my childhood friend, was a sickle-cell anemic, and when a crisis would hit, we never knew if this would be the last go-around for her. She would often say, "Don't worry about me. I'm not going anywhere until God is finished with me." And so it was! Everything the doctors said she wouldn't do, she did. And everything they said she would be, she wasn't.

But what intrigued me most was her deep, personal relationship with the Lord Jesus Christ at a young age. I had accepted the Lord Jesus at a young age too. I was six years old when I had prayed with my Sunday school teacher the prayer of salvation. I, too, had been faced with a life-threatening disease (spinal meningitis) at the age of three and almost died. The difference was, I struggled with my identity and self-esteem. As a result, I became an introverted, shy little girl.

Gloria, the outgoing dynamo, and Madeline, the quiet, bashful one, made quite a pair. We wanted to be together as much as possible. Despite outward appearances, we were soulmates and found ourselves sharing everything in our lives: our inquisitiveness about boys, our bedrooms when we spent the night at each other's houses, our dreams of singing professionally, and on and on.

Gloria believed her dreams would come true one day. I just fantasized what it would be like to experience such things. But one thing we definitely did experience together was puberty. We talked and laughed and questioned every new discovery about our bodies. Of course, Gloria was more explicit in her discussion than I, but I thank God I had a good friend to talk to about sexuality. The secrets we shared—and swore each other to confidentiality—bonded us even more.

One of the scariest days we shared occurred when we were grown up. I call it "resurrection day." Gloria had married, given birth to a beautiful daughter (something the doctors said she would never be able to do), and later was divorced. Then one day I received a call from her mother telling me Gloria had gone into a sickle cell crisis and was in the intensive care unit.

When Carl, a mutual friend, and I arrived, she was heavily sedated and semi-comatose. Carl began to read from the Psalms, and I quietly prayed and placed my right hand on Gloria's arm. After a while, she stirred a little as she began to respond to the Word and the prayer. Then, tearfully, she began to sing, "His eye is on the sparrow, and I know he watches me."

Carl and I were stunned. I began to pray with more fervor and ran my hands down her frail, little body. To my surprise, she began to climb out of bed.

"Where are you going?" I asked.

"Sick and dying people are on this floor that I need to pray for."

"Should I call the nurse? After all, you do have an IV in your arm."

With a smile, she answered, "If you want."

The nurse came in while I was helping Gloria put on her robe and slippers. "Well, lookie here! You're feeling awfully spunky," the nurse observed.

"Excuse me, but she wants to go pray for people on the floor. Is that all right?" I asked, the timid one as usual.

The nurse took Gloria's temperature and replied, "Well, your fever is broken and back to normal. Don't let me stop you."

So off we went, IV and all, rolling down the hall from one room to another. Life began to stir throughout that ward as Gloria shared her testimony and prayed with patient after patient. The place soon became noisy as people wanted to get out of bed and as nurses were called to feed suddenly hungry patients. God's power was flowing through that ward because of the frail vessel who was bolder than a lion.

The more Gloria shared, the stronger she became. Within two days, she was released from the hospital, having left her mark for God as only she could.

After that experience, I knew that death would never take my friend from me until, as she had always proclaimed, her work was finished. That work was accomplished in 1993, when Gloria died of liver dysfunction. Now, when I get to heaven, I look forward to seeing Gloria again. And I know just where to look for her. As bold as ever, she'll be somewhere close to the throne.

madeline manning mims

madeline is the only american woman to win an olympic gold medal in track for the 800-meter run. she has been a member of four u.s. olympic teams. she heads ambassador-ship, inc., through which she shares god's love using sports and the performing arts. an ordained minister and contemporary recording artist, madeline lives in tulsa, oklahoma, with her husband and their two children.

Part three

✦ moments of childhood friendship ✦

Terry Meeuswen

♦ ♦ ♦

"A friend is someone who learns how to tie her shoelaces first—and then helps you."
—Unknown

teRRy meeuwseN

no woRk, no pLay!

rowing up, I was a city kid, even though my "city"—DePere, Wisconsin—had a population of only ten thousand people. The city was divided by a river into east-side and west-side communities. In the winter, I remember walking through the dark and cold of night to the city park to skate with my friends, totally secure and confident of my safety.

But Saturdays in the summer are what I remember most fondly. Though I'm not an early riser, I would be up early enough to accomplish the obligatory task of cleaning my room. My mom was a stickler about that. No work, no play! When I knew the room would pass her inspection, I hurried to pack a bag lunch and head out for the day.

A dozen or more of us girls would pedal our bikes to our first stop: the grocery store for chicken livers and day-old bread. Not for us, but for the crabs. Then we would bike across town and out into the country till we reached a creek that meandered through rich farmland. With our bikes stowed along the embankment leading down to the stream, we would build a roughly assembled raft and take turns poling around the creek. We tied the livers to string and caught small crabs. Occasionally, a shriek would pierce the air as someone pulled up a menacing snapping turtle.

Few of us made it through the day without getting pushed off the raft. So you can imagine what we looked like by day's end. Exhausted, wet, and muddy, we would head home with buckets of crabs and dozens of stories to relate to our families.

Those were days of giggled secrets, bubbly laughter, and emerging self-sufficiency. God was in His heaven and all was right with my world.

Nostalgia is seeping into me as I write because I realize my children will never have the same luxury of freedom and sense of security I did. The world is a very different place today. Oh, to be sure, much of the change is good. I think it's wonderful to be able to see and understand our neighbors in other parts of the world, as we can through television and other news sources. Kids today know so much more about political and social happenings than I did. I think it's great we travel more and can communicate long-distance frequently and effectively.

But we've lost a simplicity that made life such an enjoyable adventure. Today I'm not comfortable with my kids riding their bikes beyond our subdivision. The roads are busy, people are in a hurry, and not everyone can be trusted.

I know my children will have their own childhood memories. But how I wish they could spend a long, lazy Saturday on a wobbly raft with a group of friends, where they could gaze into the ripples of a stream, straining to see the next big catch.

Other women's childhood memories fill the pages that follow in this section. Some of the reminiscences are of adult friends, others are of young girlfriends who were just as fun-loving, gullible, and lovable as the narrators. These are the stories of how friends shaped each other's lives in those moments of sharing heartfelt devotion to each other.

willie mae

illie Mae or GG (for Grandmother Gaston) wasn't a typical friend. Doesn't it say somewhere you're not supposed to be friends with your relatives? Well, she and I broke the rules.

Willie Mae hadn't driven since the Model T. She had no stated reason for her decision not to drive, but she was firm about it. So she rode the bus everywhere. And since Daddy was GG's only child, she spent a lot of time riding the bus to be with us.

From Willie Mae's house in downtown Atlanta to our house fifteen miles away in the suburb of Forest Park, GG took the #16 Sylvan Hills bus or the #27 Hapeville from Five Points. Then she had to catch the #54 Forest Park by 5:00 P.M.; otherwise she would have to walk from South Avenue to our home. The buses came by her house every eight minutes, but they only ran once an hour to Forest Park. She had to board the bus across from the Krystal Burger at Auburn and Peachtree (Dr. King's old stompin' grounds) to avoid standing all the way to Blair Village with her arm going numb from clinging to the overhead rail.

GG's whole life was chained to a bus schedule, but she didn't mind in the least. Many a leisurely Sunday afternoon we would ride different routes to the end of the line and back just "for the sights."

It sounds rather boring, I guess, but Willie Mae was anything but dull. Of all the people who have painted on the canvas of my life, sweet Grandmother Gaston made most of the really interesting squiggles. There was nothing she couldn't and didn't do (other than driving), and nothing and no one could stop her once she set her mind to something. No, she didn't teach me the finer points of sub-

Cathy Riso with GG (Grandmother Gaston)

mission, but she sure taught me how to grab hold of life and live it for all it was worth— no fear, no fault. Willie Mae not only gave me wings, she also showed me how to use them.

She was an honest, hard-working upholstery seamstress. I had many a skirt, jumper, and purse made of Naugahyde with a stain-retardant finish.

When GG was coming to visit, she would call at 4:30 P.M. Friday afternoon to say she was leaving her house. At 6:05 P.M. I'd go outside to sit on the front stoop to watch. Over the crest of the hill she would appear, a Rich's Department Store shopping bag in each hand. She gingerly lumbered from side-to-side on that final stretch to our house, the #54 Forest Park bus having dropped her off on its last trip to the end of the line.

Sometimes I'd run to meet her, grasping a finger released from her shopping bag grip. Sometimes I'd ride my bike and cycle round and round her, talking a mile a minute.

GG would spend the night in Forest Park about every weekend I didn't stay at her house. She slept with me. I can remember torturous nights of awakening with a desperate urge to relieve myself, only to discover that both my legs were pinned under one of hers. I'd wriggle and slither out, frantically searching in the dark for the door, making it just in time.

She also snored. Wow, did she snore! If I didn't doze off before she did, I had to finagle a way to get her to stop long enough for me to go to sleep. Eventually I found that I could hold her nose to wake her up so I could fall off to sleep. She never knew.

When I went to Willie Mae's, Mother would put me on the bus Saturday morning in Forest Park or Daddy would drive me into Atlanta Friday night. She and I shopped on Saturdays at Rich's for fabric to make lots of "fashions" she had seen in her *Photoplay* magazine. Then we took off to Newberry's Department Store to buy piano sheet music and finally ended up at the Eagle Café for lunch. I always had the beef tenderloin with gravy and two vegetables, but Willie Mae would order lots of different things. Once she even ate pigs' feet!

Newberry's, the Eagle Café, even our bus stop—they're all gone now. Construction for the '96 Olympics finished off those childhood locales, but nothing will ever erase the future that my past with Willie Mae gave me.

I suppose the greatest contribution she made to me will seem ridiculous to most. She bought me my first bra. Of course, I didn't need it. You don't need one if you have to buy an all elastic thing, but everybody else in my gym class was wearing one. Despite my father's declaration I shouldn't be controlled by what other girls did, it wasn't easy being the only braless girl. At age twelve, I was flat-chested and had no shape—just long legs, bushy eyebrows, and Naugahyde skirts. I couldn't catch a boy or a baseball; I was a bookworm. But Willie Mae gave me some much-needed dignity by buying that bra.

She was feisty. She watched *Live Atlanta Wrestling* while either reading *Photoplay* magazine or a Harlequin romance, crocheting, or eating Napoleon ice cream. It wasn't until I went off to college that I discovered Napoleon ice cream didn't exist. But I still think Napoleon tastes a little better than Neapolitan.

Willie Mae was mugged once. The police said they felt sorry for the guy. By the time they arrived on the scene, GG had chased the man down and was beating him over the head with her umbrella.

I guess she doesn't sound like a very great role model. You would have loved her, though, I promise. She was the essence of life, the essence of love. Every day, in a subtle, forthright way—or in the most dogmatic way when she felt it necessary—she lived out Jesus in front of me. She didn't beat me up with Him, but she lived her commitment to Him. She wasn't perfect; I think even I realized that. But why spoil a good thing? She was Willie Mae, "fearfully and wonderfully made."

She was my best friend. Oh, sure, Janice Presley and Joannie Morris lived up the street, but we only played together. GG and I lived life together because we shared our hearts with each other. She treated an impressionable young girl as if she were the most important human being on the planet.

When she died from a series of strokes in 1976, Daddy let me "dress" her casket. She never took well to "frou frou" stuff so I bought a big tray of her favorite African violets in pinks and purples, and I stayed up all night to crochet a blanket for her.

I'm looking forward to seeing her again. I hope she'll like how I turned out. I know she will be crazy about her great-grandbabies, and they'll finally understand why I'm so weird.

Willie Mae never had money; she spent it all on us. She didn't leave a houseful of antiques—just a bed, a shelf of Harlequin romances, and her old Singer treadle sewing machine. I inherited the brown pop-bead necklace I'd given her for Christmas when I was five, her tattered paper Bible, a lifetime of dreams and hopes, and a fire that she had sown so diligently into every seam of my life.

cathy RISO

cathy and her husband, rick, minister through music concerts at conventions, seminars, and retreats as well as in churches. cathy's professional life has run the gamut from theatrical performances to touring work with such notables as julio iglesias and placido domingo, to studio recording work, to serving as co-worship leader with rick on hosanna integrity's *as for my house*. cathy has written songs for integrity music, having performed on more than twenty of its projects. the risos live in northridge, california, with their three children.

◆ ◆ ◆

"The best and most beautiful things
in the world cannot be seen or even touched.
They must be felt with the heart."
—Helen Keller

the move to mars and venus

pressed my little nose against the car's rear window. If it had been possible, I would have pushed my face through the glass, just for a better view. (It was probably the last time my nose would qualify as "little." From that year on, it grew twice as fast as any other body part!)

What was the object of this four year old's fervent interest? Well, I really didn't know. The only thing my mother told me was that this phenomenal creature was something called "Marlyn."

You see, my mother and daddy had been traveling as evangelists in the Deep South since their wedding some nine years before. Recently, they had been offered their first pastorate, which would give stability to their two young children and provide my parents with their first weekly salary, a princely sum of forty dollars!

My parents tried to make everything seem like an adventure— even suffering. But for me, this move to the foreign soil of Midland, Pennsylvania, might just as well have been relocating to Mars.

We recently had settled into our new home, where I tried to stay out from underfoot while Mom unpacked. Of course, the only items my parents owned were a hideous floral sofa, which smelled like too many elderly, incontinent people had sat on it, and a set of aluminum glasses that was slowly poisoning us all.

But on this day I sat in the car outside the school looking for a glimpse of "Marlyn." "There she is," cried her mother, who was meeting Marlyn with us. Intently I watched each child's face and then dismissed each one until finally . . . there she was! No one had to tell me which little angel was Marlyn. She was the most beautiful girl I'd ever seen. Blonde, brown-eyed, tall, and skinny, flat feet pointed outward. At five and a half and already approaching kindergarten graduation, she soon regaled us with her playground experiences as I sat in awe. Every word was spoken with drama and animation.

Maryln Brown DeFoggi and her younger friend Cathy Rothert Lechner.

I decided that day Marlyn was my new best friend. She was, in fact, my *only* friend. But when you have just moved to Mars . . .

Soon it was Marlyn at my first birthday party in this strange new city. Then it was Marlyn who sat with me in church and Sunday school. And it was Marlyn who wept with me when she was, against her will, promoted by age to her new Sunday school class. Everything that I could possibly do with Marlyn I did.

Then, when I was seven years old, Marlyn gave me a truly wonderful gift. I was invited to become a Brownie (along with fourteen billion other hopeful seven year olds). But as the day approached for the induction ceremony followed by the mother-daughter tea, I wasn't as thrilled as I had thought I would be. We had to wear a full Brownie uniform to participate in the event. At seven, you can't comprehend that your parents can't afford the Brownie dress,

Brownie beanie, Brownie socks, Brownie belt with detachable coin purse (to hold your weekly dime dues), and coordinating shoes. I can close my eyes and still remember the painful wince on my daddy's face as I reminded him of the big Brownie countdown. It looked pretty hopeless right up until the afternoon of the tea . . . that is, until Marlyn stepped in.

My mother drove me to my friend's house and there, hanging neatly pressed in her closet, was her Brownie dress, beanie, socks, and belt with detachable coin purse, which she bequeathed to me. What a great God; what an awesome friend.

Marlyn loved her God. Jesus was her Jesus, and she knew Him in a way that called me to a deeper place. I loved Jesus as Marlyn did.

Then, in 1963, tragedy struck. No, no one died, but it sure felt like it. My father accepted the pastorate of a church on the other end of the state. It might as well have been Venus, as far as I was concerned.

The good news was that, if Cathy and Marlyn were David and Jonathan, our mothers were Ruth and Naomi, and our fathers . . . maybe Wally and the Beaver?

Each summer after we moved, Marlyn's parents and mine planned a two-week vacation together. Our families would rendezvous to camp. I had no clue this recreation was chosen because we had no money. I thought our parents selected it because they hated us.

When the Browns and the Rotherts would gather once a year to plan the vacation, we preteen girls had a different agenda than our parents. Our mothers would make menu lists, and our fathers would pull out nation-sized maps to plan a route that would inevitably include a 3:00 A.M. departure with as few stops along the way as possible. Bathroom stops were grudgingly accommodated as long as we would sign an affidavit swearing we could not hold it another forty-six miles.

But the moment Marlyn and I said our first hellos, we would sneak off to an upstairs bedroom, an attic corner, or on several occasions a cramped closet where we would pray. Baby dolls, Barbie,

Ken, Midge, Skipper, the latest *haute couture* for the twelve-inch doll set, were packed away. Praying rather than playing was our keen desire.

Now, I know what you're thinking: That isn't normal. But just like Elizabeth, the mother of John the Baptist, and Mary, the girl-woman who bore our Lord Jesus, when Marlyn and I saw each other, after a year of furtive letter writing, we both wanted to pray. Within five minutes our little spirits were crying out to God in deep intercession for our generation, our husbands to come, the nations, and our husbands to come. We could hear our mothers sneak up on us to listen. At times they believed we were strange.

One year we added an activity to our reunion. Though we knew nothing about the biblical principle of the "blood covenant," up in the attic we pricked our forefingers (Marlyn's idea) and solemnly swore. Marlyn insisted on solemnity and secrecy. In fact, after you read this, you must eat the pages so Marlyn doesn't find out I told! The only problem is I can't remember what our solemn, secret vow was . . .

I loved my Marlyn. I had plenty of new friends to play with in the new churches, in the new schools, and scattered among my countless school activities. But my Marlyn grabbed my hand and took me higher. We both took piano lessons, voice lessons, and the requisite worthless math classes. But Marlyn was just better—at everything. Yet we were never competitive nor jealous. When two people have shared the intimacy of the prayer closet, there forms an unearthly bond that rejoices in God's obvious blessing on each other's lives.

Our teenage years brought the usual angst. We fell in and out of love regularly. But one thing was certain. We would marry uncompromising, romantic, and gorgeous men of God.

By then our summer vacation planning sessions were used to practice church services. In Marlyn's basement a rough church was set up, and we took turns preaching and leading worship. Even our poor little goofball brothers, who had for years been barred from our private ceremonies, became willing, if somewhat squirmy, congregational members.

I was there when Marlyn began to fall in love with an older, tall, handsome Italian preacher's son who was attending Bible school. That was the summer before her senior year in high school, and together we cried out and sought our best friend, the precious Holy Spirit, to speak and to lead. I still have the Christmas letter she sent me, telling me she simply couldn't live without Paul; he had asked her to be his wife and partner in ministry.

If I close my eyes and get really quiet, I can see my Marlyn walking down the aisle to join her Paul twenty-seven years ago. As her best friend and maid of honor, I was fulfilling a promise we had made to each other fifteen years before. But a certain sadness was inevitable, I guess. I was giving my sister not only to another but also to a new life.

Five years later, Marlyn came to Florida so she could stand at my side as my matron of honor when I gave myself to a tall, handsome Jewish man. Marlyn had kept me up the entire night before with illustrations and Tim and Beverly LaHaye books, preparing me for the intimate side of marriage.

I can only remember one time in all those years that Marlyn was really mad at me. It was the summer of '67 (not that I'm keeping track). That was the year I developed breasts and she didn't! But that was also the year she got long legs . . . and I didn't. Where's the justice?

The life of a pastor's family is filled with change, but God, in His grace, gave me a friend from childhood to womanhood.

Marlyn Brown DeFoggi, you have been wife, mother, pastor's wife, teacher, church secretary, missionary, and now author. But even before you were any of these, you were a lover of God and my best friend.

this friendship reminds me of . . .

❏ the day you gave me a wonderful gift

❏ the way we shared our faith together

❏ the day you grabbed my hand and took me higher

❏ the day you walked down the aisle to meet your bridegroom

❏ the moments of prayer we shared with each other

❏ the day we pricked our forefingers and solemnly swore . . .

_____

_____

_____

cathy Lechner

cathy speaks at women's conferences and churches across the country and in many foreign countries. she is the author of three best-selling books, *i want to sit at his feet, but who's going to cook dinner?*, *can't we just kill 'em and tell god they died?*, and *i hope god's promises come to pass before my body parts go south*. her husband, randi, is a minister; they have seven children and live in jacksonville, florida.

SUNDAY SISTER

 met my best friend, Jackie Smith, when I was nine years old. She came with her parents to my father's church in Brooklyn, New York. Jackie always sat toward the front of the church, between her mom and dad. I sat on the side aisle and we stared at each other but were too shy to speak. Finally, after several months, our fathers introduced us to each other at the back of the church near the coatrack. That inauspicious beginning started a friendship that will last forever, as far as we're concerned.

Right away we realized we shared lots of interests. We began to spend Sundays together, starting with the morning service and concluding with the evening meeting. We constantly talked about the Lord and sang hymns and choruses together.

At first, we would ask our dads for ten cents to buy candy after the morning service. Then this amount changed to two dollars when we grew a little older and discovered Richelleu, a quaint little restaurant nearby. We were to spend many Sundays there absorbed in girl talk. Our conversations were about boys, our dreams, and our special desire to find and do God's will. In fact, as the years brought us closer together, our spiritual hunger formed the center of our friendship.

After eating we would take walks around the neighborhood and later return to the church to spend the rest of the afternoon playing the piano, singing, and praying for the evening service.

Since our relationship revolved around the church, we were thrilled when one day, as I visited Jackie's home, we walked into her bedroom to find identical dresses her mother had purchased so we could look like sisters on Sundays.

For several months during our early teenage years, God caused people in our church to feel a new hunger to know and love Jesus. Church members would find themselves at the altar till one or two in the morning, only to return the next night eager to wait in God's presence. We teens became bold witnesses in our schools. We couldn't keep our mouths shut! We just had to tell others about Jesus' love, and many came to know the Lord as a result. Because Jackie and I experienced this revival together, the spiritual bond of our friendship grew deeper.

As years passed, we talked about all the changes involved with growing up. Laughter, tears, and a constant stream of prayerful concern flowed between us right through high school. During one of those talks I shared with Jackie my desire to be in full-time music ministry and to direct a choir. And one Sunday I informed my best friend I had a crush on Jim Cymbala, my brother's best friend. He would later become my sweetheart and then my husband. Jackie, of course, shared in our wedding as the maid of honor.

After marriage my husband and I felt called to the ministry, even though neither of us was trained formally. Soon we found ourselves pastoring a tiny, struggling church in Brooklyn. Jackie, who was living with her parents in Brooklyn, was busy as a grade school teacher and in leadership in the church she attended. Still, our deep friendship was somehow maintained, even though our busy lives kept us from being together as often as in the past. When we did speak on the phone or meet on a Saturday afternoon, the special bond was still there. We both felt free to open our hearts to laugh, to cry, and to pray together.

Now, who would ever dream that seven years ago Jackie would come to our church to work side by side with my husband and me? Who could have dreamed that, after her parents passed away, God would relocate her to a beautiful co-op just one mile from my home?

Jackie now helps in our music program and sings in the choir I direct. And together we watch God faithfully fulfill dreams we prayed about decades ago. My Sunday sister remains that true friend who is there for me—no matter what—every day of the week.

Carol
Cymbala
and
Jackie
Smith

carol cymbala

carol's girlhood dream of directing a choir and having a ministry through music has resulted in her receiving one dove award and several dove nominations. she was given two grammy awards for "best gospel album by a choir or chorus" in 1993 and 1995 and nominated five other times for grammy awards. carol now directs a 240-voice choir in the once tiny inner-city church she and her husband started, the brooklyn tabernacle. she and jim have three children and four grandchildren.

can you reach my friend?

met my best friend, Valerie Hood, way back in 1967 when we were pint-sized. Because we were inseparable, we were nicknamed Salt and Pepper. Everyone in elementary, junior high, and high school knew we were better than sisters . . . we were true friends.

When we had disagreements, even as far back as grade school, we never spoke an ill word about each other to anyone during those "mad" times. We cared too much to say bad things.

As little girls, we would go into retail stores and talk in a made-up language that no one understood—including us. People would look at us as if we were strange, which caused us to laugh so hard we cried. I can still picture us giggling and holding our sides from all that laughter as we rushed out of the store.

In 1980, when Val and I were teens, my family moved to Tennessee from the 'hood of Cleveland, Ohio. Without my friend I felt so alone. I graduated from high school and went on to college. Then, my freshman year, I found what true love was all about. I found Jesus, and I found with Him I could have peace and joy— not just happiness.

Although Valerie didn't get the educational breaks I did, she cheered me on. When I received Christ, she was confused but happy for my joy. When I got married to Reggie White, she supported me. When I had my children, she was there. Those were hard years for her, but she was always there for me, sharing my blessings.

Well, today I'm proud to say Val has become a Christian, a lovely wife to Terrence Fletcher, and a wonderful mother to Alexis Jecolia and Taylor Marie. She named her first daughter after my daughter, Jecolia, which means "most powerful." That's what we plan for our girls, to be powerful.

Although demographics limited our time together after we were sixteen, our hearts were always together. Even today as thirty-plus gals, we still have crazy fun in public. We like to listen to people talk about how they know my husband and me—but they don't! I never tell them I am the woman they claim to know. Val edges into the conversation by asking them questions: "What did you think of Jecolia's incident on her bike?" or "You heard about Reggie's accident in the bathtub, didn't you?" Despite neither incident nor accident being true, these people make up answers! Val and I struggle not to break into giggles that hurt our sides as we rush away from the conversation. We're just a couple of carefree comedians—always have been.

But Valerie has taught me so much more than how to have a good laugh. After I was married, I realized I had a temper and I was bossy. Val had put up with my bossiness for more than two decades but had quietly concentrated on loving my outgoing personality. Thankfully for all involved, God delivered me from that bossy spirit.

Now we see each other once or twice a year. Life is so short and visits don't come often enough. We have to make time for each other and to make memories.

Now we can sit and chat about how great God is and what He is doing in our lives. It means a lot to me that my best friend has dedicated her life to the Lord. After I became a Christian, I sang a song, "Can You Reach My Friend?," and each time I sang, I prayed for Valerie . . . look at God, He reached her one thousand miles away!

sara white

while attending col-lege, sara met her husband, reggie white, future hall of fame defensive lineman for the green bay packers. sara utilizes her degrees in marketing and management by being involved in a myriad of entrepreneurial projects including urban hope, a nonprofit ministry offering hope to inner city and rural residents. she is also the cohost of *sports cooking*, a tv cooking show featuring prominent celebrities from across the nation. she can also be seen in "sara 101," a weekly segment which is part of reggie's *inside rush* television show. she and reggie have two children and have helped to raise two boys and several fos-ter children.

Valerie Hood-Fletcher

Part four

✦ moments of comfort ✦

"Aunt Linda" enveloped by the whole family—Christmas, 1992

terry meeuwsen

aunt Linda

fter years of singing in the nightclub circuit, a
year of travel as Miss America, and numerous
public relations stints, I was finally going to set-
tle down in Milwaukee, Wisconsin, where my
husband was involved in business. The opportunity to establish a
home of my own and to travel a little less was appealing. Although
I had a couple of special friends in the area, they were at different
places in their lives—very busy with business and family.

As a young Christian, I knew I needed to get established in a
local Bible study to grow in the Lord as well as for encouragement
and accountability. In the five years since I had committed my life
to Christ, I hadn't been in one place long enough to establish deep
friendships with believers. It wasn't something I missed because I'd
never had it.

Somewhere along the way, I had learned of a nondenomina-
tional group called Christian Women's Club. I knew they must
have a group that met in my area. After discovering the name of a
woman in leadership, I called, introduced myself, and was invited
to attend a Bible study. At the study, I learned of an outreach about
to begin in Milwaukee called "Here's Life," and they needed volunteers. I thought, *Okay, Lord, use me!* I had no idea what I was

qualified to do nor what the program needed. I was willing to address envelopes, make phone calls, or make coffee—it didn't matter.

When I arrived at the planning session, I was told that along with a woman named Linda Strom I would conduct meetings on how to pray. We would travel together by car to churches all over southeastern Wisconsin. I wondered what Linda, my partner in prayer, would be like.

Over the next several months, we drove for hours, often losing our way, with plenty of time to get to know each other. At each church, I would share my testimony and sing while Linda would teach on prayer. We were both going through some intense testing in our personal lives. On the way to and from the churches, we would share our thoughts and feelings, laugh, cry, and pray for each other. Out of that time together a friendship was forged that has touched every area of my life.

The next few years brought unimagined marital conflict that finally ended in divorce. It was a humiliating and painful time, but also a time of soul-searching and surrender. Through it all, Linda was there. When I grieved, she grieved with me. Though her own life was busy, she was always available to walk, talk, or pray. Sometimes we did all three.

Linda knows everything there is to know about me and loves me anyway. We have walked together through more valleys and victories than I can count. But the thing I love the most about Linda is how consistently she reflects Jesus in her life. Being her friend has drawn me to a deeper place in the Lord. She sees people the way Jesus does. Linda has taken me into the heart of the inner city, to hospitals, prisons, retirement homes, boardrooms, executive mansions, and poverty-ridden apartments. You see, Linda, like Jesus, is no respecter of persons. Nothing in life thrills her more than sharing with someone the awesome good news that Jesus came to set the captives free. I think that's why people are drawn to her. She could care less what you have or what you do. She's genuinely interested in your heart and soul.

My children call her "Aunt Linda," which is appropriate because she is family. Linda and her husband, Dallas, married Andy and me and baptized all four of our children. Linda and I have rejoiced in new beginnings and mourned the death of dreams. We aren't necessarily alike, but our hearts, minds, and spirits are inextricably joined together.

Though it's painful to not see each other regularly since Andy and I have moved to Virginia, the distance has made me appreciate more fully my God-given friend. I wish everyone could experience the kind of friendship we have. It's a rare gift and I am so thankful!

In the stories that follow, women acknowledge with heartfelt gratitude friends who stood with them in difficult times and offered the kind of tender loving care and understanding that only a true friend can give. We'll begin with Linda Strom's version of our blessed friendship.

♦ ♦ ♦

"Friends are amazing—
they know you well and still like you!"
—Samuel, age twelve

Linda Strom with Terry Meeuwsen

a gift beyond measure

s I reflect back on my life, I can see how God, like a magnificent conductor, orchestrates relationships to enlarge our understanding of His grace. Growing up on a battlefield, with an alcoholic father and an unhappy mother, I was on a quest for peace and a sense of belonging. In 1964 I found what I was looking for through a relationship with Jesus Christ.

Then, in 1973 God led my husband, Dallas, and me to Milwaukee. The move was difficult for our three young boys. We may have been in full-time ministry, but our family was in trouble. At fifteen, Terry, our oldest son, slowly drifted away to a place known as the Far Country. Fear gradually choked out all my expectations that this journey would ever end.

I appreciated the disciples' accounts of the storm-tossed Sea of Galilee. Oh, sure, I understood the facts and how they applied to me. Jesus might have been in my boat, but I longed for still waters. Dallas and I felt frustrated, discouraged, and disappointed. Had we missed God's will in this move to Milwaukee? Were we disqualified from serving Him?

In the midst of these pain-racked questions, in 1975 Terry Meeuwsen and I were teamed up to conduct prayer seminars associated with a city-wide evangelistic campaign. I have to admit I was intimidated. We were an unlikely duo. She had just returned to Wisconsin after an exciting and challenging year traveling around the world as Miss America. I had moved from Minneapolis in a U-Haul. She was the most beautiful woman I had ever seen; I was working on softening my dishpan hands. I had three sons; she had Samson and Delilah, her two Shitzu dogs. Our only common ground was love and appreciation for Jesus Christ. But that was all we needed to build a friendship that has continued to grow for more than twenty years.

After we taught on prayer in various churches in the area, we would leave the seminars and pray for one another in the car. We felt free to share openly on any subject.

One night we stopped at a local pie shop to eat a piece of fabulous strawberry pie. I was recounting my latest episode with my mother in great detail and with unreserved emotion. Terry looked me straight in the eye and said, "When you talk about your mother, Linny, it's different than when you talk about anything else. You really need to deal with this." I stopped eating. My pie was ruined; I knew my friend had spoken the truth.

Several days passed before I allowed the Holy Spirit access to all the pain and anger I felt over past hurts with Mom. God forgave me, and with that forgiveness I had new strength to forgive my mother. Deep hurt had festered in my heart since childhood, but Jesus placed His wounded hand on my broken heart and began the healing process.

Then an unexpected miracle happened. My mother received Jesus into her life. Receiving Christ into one's life is one thing; cooperating with the Lord to bring emotional health and peace is another. Mom has continued to be a tool in God's hands to reveal unyielded areas in my life.

One Christmas Terry gave me a needlepoint pillow with these hand-stitched words: "If it's not one thing it's your mother." Too true. The pillow makes me smile even as it reminds me of the truth it proclaims.

The foundation of our friendship is Jesus Christ. Prayer is the connection with Him and each other.

Humor and truth are the building blocks in my friendship with Terry. I can't think of one serious situation we've cried over that we haven't also laughed over. And even though I started our relationship thinking we couldn't be more different, God showed me our hearts were a match.

Terry sings "Somebody Prayed for Me," a song that expresses what real friendship exhibits.

> Someone took my heart to heaven on bended knee,
> Somebody wouldn't stop believing till God had met my need
> And I'm stronger today 'cause somebody prayed for me.

I'm stronger today, and so is our oldest son, the one who took the journey into the Far Country. Long ago, on bended knee, Terry and I prayed for his return. Last year the three of us ministered together at a "Healing for Your Heart" conference. It was a mother's dream come true.

Linda Strom

Linda Strom and her husband, Dallas, founded Discipleship Unlimited, a ministry designed "for the equipping of the saints for the work of ministry" (Eph. 4:12). Together they teach others how to conduct marriage seminars, hold weekly interdenominational Bible studies, and coordinate ministries to inmates in prisons. They live in Milwaukee and have three sons and two grandsons.

ORDINARY PEOPLE

 t was boring at times, I'm sure, to greet people at the church door. Sometimes the couple who had assumed that chore probably weren't in the mood to hug people; other times they might have preferred just to hide in a pew. But sometimes God places His people in mundane jobs so they can fulfill some special purpose.

As a teenager, I was one of those visitors who passed by the greeters of Community Baptist Church in Manhattan Beach, California. The couple had a skill they applied liberally: They knew how to hug someone who wasn't sure she wanted to be hugged. Shorty and Villa Croft were their names—or Mom and Dad Croft, as everyone called them. This dear couple had decided no matter what humdrum job they took in the church, they would do it heartily.

After several weeks of bear hugs, these greeters figured out they were hugging a single, pregnant girl. I was finding it harder to hide my pregnancy. And harder to answer the questions—not only from others but also from myself, questions that haunted me at night. Would anyone believe I was pregnant as a result of a rape? But rape only happens to bad girls, right? Would people scorn me? What did all this mean about my baby? Why did God let this happen?

Originally, I had moved from my alcoholic home in Philadelphia to San Francisco when I was fresh out of high school. To complicate things further, I was a new convert, a decision I had made at a Billy Graham Crusade.

The night I was raped by a fellow worker I was devastated. Then I discovered I was pregnant. Because an abortion in Mexico wasn't an appealing option, I had time to seek God.

And the Lord had time to show me that abortion is too permanent an answer to a temporary problem. After all, my father had told me I was an unwanted child. If Scripture was true, even though a couple may decide to make love, it is God who decides to make life. I reasoned that God had wanted me born, and apparently God wanted this life in me born also.

So I had decided to escape to Southern California. Then the Lord hugged me, using the arms and hearts of Mom and Dad Croft. After some months, in her distinctive Southern drawl, Mom said, "Dad and me are fixin' to ask y'all to come live with us; we can tell a girl who needs a square meal and a good home."

Living with the Crofts meant being squeezed into a little house along with their sweet daughter, Carol, and her two little boys. It was a blast. We all fit in somehow, shared bathrooms, and rejoiced in the love that made us a family. In this loving atmosphere I opted for adoption and relinquished my baby girl. The birth day was tough because I simply signed papers and never saw nor held my child. I consoled myself by thinking I'd have plenty of other children. I couldn't imagine that would be the only child to whom I would give birth.

The love and friendship of the Croft family helped to heal my wounds. And the lives of these two "just greeters" warms my heart to this day. These ordinary people helped to convince me that you can still trust God even when you can't see Him. Knowing that adoption records were sealed in California, I closed that chapter of my life.

Twenty years later, the Crofts sat in their same worn recliners in that same little house when the phone rang. A female voice said to Dad Croft, "I'm looking for Lee Kinney, do you know her?"

Intuitively Dad knew this was my baby and nervously blurted out, "Lee Kinney . . . well, we used to know her, but we don't anymore . . . er . . . she moved . . ."

Mom Croft grabbed the phone. "Why are you looking for Lee?" The sweet voice, calling from Michigan, announced she was my birth daughter and had been searching for me for years. This was her last hope of finding me. Could they help?

In the wisdom that only comes from knowing God, Mom Croft said that if this gal would write a letter, Mom would try to pass it on to me. No promises.

When Mom Croft received the letter, she called me and left a message on my answering machine. She nervously said, "Hey, hon, we got a call from your baby . . . I know this is sudden. We didn't want to mess up your life or anything so we didn't call you. But now we got this letter . . . and it is so beautiful! Call us."

I fell back in my chair on hearing the words "your baby." I called right away, and we cried together on the phone. Mom put the letter in the mail to me.

The day I received the letter I called the mystery phone number in Michigan. The charming voice that answered belonged to Julie Makimaa. Since then we have reunited, and I've had the joyous fun of knowing my two grandchildren, Casey and Herb.

Right after Julie and I had our reunion, Mom and Dad Croft went into rest homes. The phone number Julie called was disconnected after forty years. Had her call come a few weeks later, she would have had no success.

Shortly after that Dad Croft went home to be with Jesus. But I wanted Mom Croft to meet Julie face-to-face. So Julie and I sneaked into the rest home after hours just before Julie caught a flight back to Michigan.

Mom looked so frail and delicate, in spite of her size. We tiptoed up to her bed. Was she sleeping? As I put my hand on her cold arm, her eyes popped open.

"Lee," she exclaimed, trying to sit up, "let me make some coffee."

"No, Mom," I said as I pushed her back. "I just wanted you to meet my baby."

Then Mom's eyes fell on Julie—a mirror image of me. Julie smiled as she cried and thanked Mom Croft for all Mom had done to help bring Julie into the world and to make our reunion a reality. We had no coffee, but we shared the Bread of Life, and prayed and thanked God for His hidden purposes and His surprise friendships.

The next day I returned to the rest home with an armful of copies of *The Missing Piece,* which told Mom Croft's story. I gave the books to all the nurses and caregivers, saying, "Don't you know you have a celebrity in room 209? She's in this book; you should be thrilled you have a star here!"

After that, I'm told, Mom Croft received special treatment. The hair stylist would come to her room and do her hair for free, if Mom would tell the story again. Often Mom would have three or four people standing in her room as she recounted the story. And there wouldn't be a dry eye in the place.

I'm deeply indebted to those two senior citizens—now citizens of heaven. They would have considered themselves insignificant in the big scheme of things. But that's whom God uses to execute His extraordinary plans, ordinary people. Is it possible God is positioning you to be in just the right spot at just the right time to befriend and comfort someone in need? Watch for His purposes in your everyday life. Maybe you, too, have come to the kingdom "for such a time as this."

Lee ezell

Lee divides her time between writing and speaking, which has taken her to a variety of countries. Her books, which include *the missing piece, the cinderella syndrome,* and *will the real me please stand up,* have been translated into twelve languages. Lee is the president of ezell communications in newport beach, california.

Lee Ezell
and her friend
Villa "Mom" Croft

who was never
further away
than the
telephone.

inherit a blessing

☙

oftentimes, friends can convince us that when
we can't trace god, we can still trust him.
they become a blessing to us. and we can also
become a blessing to them.

i remember a time when you did this for me . . .

_____

_____

_____

_____

_____

_____

◆ ◆ ◆

Finally, all of you be of one mind,
having compassion for one another;
love as brothers, be tenderhearted, be courteous;
not returning evil for evil or reviling for reviling,
but on the contrary blessing, knowing that
you were called to this, that you may
inherit a blessing.
—1 Peter 3:8–9 NKJV

Evelyn Roberts and Charlotte DeWeese

♦ ♦ ♦

"People who can hold their tongues
rarely have any trouble holding their friends."
—Unknown

evelyn Roberts

the unfinished conversation

he Bible says, "There is a friend who sticks closer than a brother" (Prov. 18:24 NKJV). I found such a friend in 1950.

Charlotte DeWeese and her husband, Bob, who were in Iowa, came to Tulsa to have dinner in our home before they returned to their pastorate in Tacoma, Washington. The manager of our crusades had just retired, and he had recommended Bob take his place. So the DeWeeses came for dinner.

That evening, as Charlotte and I spent some time together away from the men, we discussed our families, our ministry, and our future. I found the DeWeeses had three sons—two of whom they had birthed and the third adopted. As we talked, I realized here was a woman I could trust and rely upon.

Soon after our visit Oral called Bob on the phone and offered him the position of manager of the crusades, and Bob accepted. Now, this meant their family would be disrupted from the pastorate where they were settled. Bob would travel to cities to ask pastors to sponsor the crusades. So Charlotte would either have to travel with Bob to every crusade or be without him for three weeks each month.

Many women would have rebelled but not Charlotte. Even though she knew her sons would be left at home, she and Bob, through prayer, decided she should travel with him. Charlotte never wavered from their decision.

She has been a woman of prayer all the years I've known her. And she's a stickler for fitting her daily devotional time into her life.

I remember once when we had a crusade in Pensacola, Florida. I decided I would walk on the beach and thought Charlotte might want to go with me. I knocked on her door and said, "Charlotte, what are you doing?" She answered, "I'm just trying to get spiritual." We've laughed over that many times.

I found I could pour out my troubles to Charlotte, and not only would she pray and counsel me, but she also kept my struggles in her heart, telling no one. I knew that what I told her went only to the Lord in prayer.

It's hard to find that kind of friend. Most people feel they are called of God to spread around some confidence you have shared with them. Because of that, many of us hold our problems inside. If we can open up, talk them out with a friend, and then pray, God gives us release, and we can go on with our lives.

Whatever problems our family had, Charlotte and Bob were always there ready to pray, to comfort us, and to lift us up. During the '70s, our son Richard was a rebellious young man. He had the call of God on his life and knew it but was running from the Lord. So many times I went to Charlotte with this heavy burden. After prayer and reading the Word of God, plus receiving encouraging words from Charlotte, I always left with an uplifted heart.

Then in 1977 we lost our daughter and son-in-law in a plane crash. One of the first to come to us (besides Collins Steele who brought us the news) were Bob and Charlotte. When our oldest son, Ronnie, died, Bob and Charlotte were by our sides. Bob did the service; what a blessing he and Charlotte were to us that day when our hearts were broken.

Charlotte had problems, too, now and then, and she felt she

could share them with me. I remember one day I was vacuuming when Charlotte called.

She said, "Evelyn, I'm in trouble. May I come see you?"

"Of course, Charlotte; come now."

When she walked into my house, she was as white as a piece of paper. I could see fear written all over her. She had just been to the doctor who found a small knot on the side of her neck below her ear. He told her more than likely it was cancer and would have to be surgically removed. But there was a high risk the nerves on one side of her face would be damaged and perhaps affect her mouth and her eye.

After she told me the problem, I said, "Charlotte, we're going to pray about that and cast out the cancer or whatever it is in Jesus' Name."

So with the vacuum sweeper in the middle of the room, we knelt, wept, and prayed, and reminded the Lord of His words. "I am the God who healeth thee" (Ex. 15:26), "By His stripes, you were healed" (1 Peter 2:24), "Ask what you will in my name and my Father in Heaven will give it to you" (John 16:23), "Where two agree as touching anything, whatever they ask shall be done by my Father in Heaven" (Matthew 18:19), and others. When we finished, I said, "Charlotte, if that was cancer, it's gone. Don't let anyone cut on your face. Talk it over with Bob and get a second opinion."

Well, she did, and she has never had surgery. That was twenty-five years ago.

Charlotte is now eighty-seven. Her Bob went to heaven several years ago. That was a hard time for her. After all, you can't live with the one you love for more than fifty years and not miss him when God calls him home. All of Charlotte's family and friends prayed for and comforted her, and she came out strong—not depressed nor down—but with her faith centered in Jesus.

Charlotte lives at University Village, a Christian retirement center owned by Oral Roberts University. I visit her as often as I can.

We still have our times of sharing and praying together. She tells me she has found a mission field there, and she is so busy ministering to the many who live at the village, it's hard to find her in her apartment. She could be resting, reading, or visiting her children and grandchildren. But she's out telling people about God's love and mercy.

Charlotte is a rare person, and I've been blessed to say she is my very best friend. The two of us have never been together long enough to feel we have completely finished a conversation. I'm looking forward to the time when we're both in our eternal home, and we can sit down under a tree to talk over all the things we've been through together. We'll have an eternity to finish our conversation.

EVELYN ROBERTS

THE WIFE OF EVANGELIST ORAL ROBERTS, EVELYN HAS TRAVELED TO MANY COUNTRIES WITH HER HUSBAND AS PART OF HIS EXTENSIVE MINISTRY AND FOUNDED ORAL ROBERTS UNIVERSITY WITH HIM. SHE IS THE AUTHOR OF SEVERAL BOOKS INCLUDING, *HIS DARLING WIFE, EVELYN* AND A CHILDREN'S BOOK, *HEAVEN HAS A FLOOR.* MARRIED SINCE 1938, THE ROBERTS ARE THE PARENTS OF FOUR CHILDREN, THIRTEEN GRANDCHILDREN, AND ONE GREAT-GRANDCHILD.

JUDY TO THE RESCUE

y friend Judy didn't set out to ensure my future marital bliss that day; all we did was pray together. But, oh, the power of praying with a friend!

I was nearing my thirtieth birthday and starting to panic. Maybe that's why I justified dating a man whose faith was shaky, and whose crooked smile made me ache with a longing that was anything but spiritual.

Judy to the rescue.

I dropped by her apartment for a casual chat that soon turned into a steady stream of tears and a sobbing confession. "I'm not sure he's God's best choice for me, but if I don't do something soon, I'm doomed!"

"Let's pray about it," Judy suggested. When she knelt by the couch, I knew this was serious stuff. Down I went, holding on tight to her hand.

Judy started with a word of thanks for our friendship, for my honesty, and for our mutual desire to seek God's will. Then it was my turn. Silence. The pain of my breaking heart was so excruciating, I could barely breathe.

Neither of us spoke for what seemed like half an hour (but was probably half a minute). Then I hesitantly began to hand over what was left of my heart to the Lord. Deep down I knew I was the one at fault, not the man in question, and I alone needed to make a wrong thing right.

Judy squeezed my hand to assure me she was with me 100 percent. "Don't be afraid, Liz," she whispered.

More tears, more repentance, more earnest prayer. Judy didn't need to say much. Just her presence and her willingness to hang in there with me through my travail were enough.

By the time we opened our eyes and stood up, the next step was clear. I had to break up with this dear man. I stopped by his place on the way home from Judy's so I wouldn't lose my resolve. In a word, it was awful.

When he married another woman a few months later, I felt even worse. Had I been mistaken after all? Was I going to be single forever because of my foolishness?

But two years later, God brought a wonderful husband of my own into my life. Then I understood the blessing of repentance and obedience, thanks to a friend's gentle comfort.

Not long after the nuptials, a good friend in almost an identical situation came to me, sobbing for relief from her dilemma. Thanks to Judy's ministry of prayer and comfort, which I had experienced firsthand, I knew exactly what to do.

"Let's pray about it," I suggested, taking her hand and heading for the couch. After all, what are friends for?

LIZ CURTIS HIGGS

LIZ HAS PRESENTED MORE THAN twelve HUNDRED HUMOROUS, ENCOURAGING PROGRAMS FOR AUDIENCES ALL ACROSS AMERICA. IN 1993 LIZ EARNED THE PRESTIGIOUS DESIGNATION OF CERTIFIED SPEAKING PROFESSIONAL. SHE IS ALSO THE AUTHOR OF TWELVE BOOKS, INCLUDING *HELP, I'M LAUGHING AND I CAN'T GET UP, ONLY ANGELS CAN WING IT, WHILE SHEPHERDS WASHED THEIR FLOCKS*, AND *MIRROR, MIRROR ON THE WALL, HAVE I GOT NEWS FOR YOU!* SHE LIVES WITH HER HUSBAND AND TWO CHILDREN IN AN OLD HOUSE IN LOUISVILLE, KENTUCKY.

Judy Rigsby

✦ ✦ ✦

"Friendship
is the only cement
which will hold the
world together."
—Unknown

✦ ✦ ✦

tHE SIX - week sacrifice

wo of my dearest friends—Kim Lancaster and Frances Foley—set aside their plans to meet an urgent need of mine in April 1989. At that time my father asked me to be with him in West Virginia during the final stages of his battle with cancer.

"How long can you stay?" he asked.

Without thinking, I replied, "Six weeks, Dad. I'll come with the children, and we'll be together every day for six weeks." I didn't know how I would arrange it, but I wanted to be with him with all my heart. After I hung up, I wondered, *Why did I say six weeks? And how do I plan to meet Dad's needs and care for my four children:* Jessica, Canaan, Christian, and Jenna were ages six, five, two, and eight months. I was still nursing Jenna.

The fellowship we enjoyed the previous two years of Dad's life had begun in a hospital room in Rochester, Minnesota. I was with him as he acknowledged his helplessness and his fear. I saw him turn to Jesus Christ and recognize Him as Lord and Savior.

During Dad's illness, Gary had driven the children and me back and forth from Florida to West Virginia so we could be with my father. And I had flown to visit him several times with the children. But this visit, I knew, would be different. Dad wanted to find a way to say good-bye. Something in the bonding time, he realized, would help him to let go of this life.

That spring my stepdaughter Kim was enrolled as a sophomore at a Bible college in Rhode Island. I called her and told her I needed to go home to be with my dad. As usual, Kim understood what mattered most in my life better than any other friend I had.

When she was living at home, we often talked until the early morning. When I was pregnant with Jenna, she had rubbed my feet. The children called her "Kimmy," and we all cried every time we said good-bye. Kim made room in her heart for me the first summer we were together, when she was only eleven.

When this crisis came up, Kim set aside her life for me. She told the dean of women about our situation, and the school gave her permission to join me in Parkersburg and to complete her exams there. We set up housekeeping in a furnished townhouse near my parents, and Kim cared for Jessica, Canaan, and Christian. My baby, Jenna, and I spent part of every morning, afternoon, and evening at the hospital.

But I still had a dilemma. I nursed Jenna every four hours. I knew I couldn't keep her with me in Dad's hospital room; yet I wasn't willing to have her far from me. I knew one person who could help me with my problem, Frances Foley.

Frances and her husband, Doug, live just up the river from Parkersburg. Gary and I had met them in a small church when we lived there in 1984. Jessica was a year old at the time, and I was pregnant with Canaan. Jessica wouldn't stay in the nursery—until we met Frances, and then being in the nursery was fun.

The days that drew Frances, Doug, and me closer than any other were those six weeks caring for my father. They counted their role in that endeavor as an assignment from the Lord and delighted in being in the hospital lobby every day to care for Jenna. After I would nurse Jenna, Frances quieted her, held her for hours, and put her to sleep.

Sometimes when I went to the lobby, people had gathered around just to watch Frances and Doug laughing and talking to the baby. When Jenna fussed, Doug would come to Dad's room to let me know. As I nursed Jenna, we talked about Dad's walk with the Lord. We praised God for the friendship that Dad and I had in Christ. Frances and Doug never wearied in doing good. They never tired of hearing the good reports about Dad's faith.

Kim and Frances manifested the fruit of the Spirit—love, joy, peace, patience, kindness, goodness, faithfulness, gentleness, and self-control. Kim, a vigorous young woman, had wisdom beyond her years. Frances, a Titus 2 woman, demonstrated strength and vitality. The commitment they both made to me and to the Lord continues to speak to me nearly a decade later. I love them with all my heart, and I praise God for placing us in each other's lives.

Dad went to be with the Lord at the very end of those six weeks. Thanks to Kim and Frances, I was with him, standing beside his bed at home, singing softly with the rest of my family as he drew his last breath.

terry dorian, ph.d.

terry is an author, conference speaker, health researcher, and an expert on the role of whole foods in the prevention and cure of degenerative diseases. her books include *Health Begins in Him*, *The Cookbook—Health Begins in Him*, *Anyone Can Home School* (with co-author, zan peters tyler), and *Hormonal Imbalance—The Madness and the Message*. terry and her husband, gary, live and homeschool their four children in hendersonville, north carolina.

the sacrifice of friendship

Terry Dorian

sometimes friends go out
of their way to meet an
urgent need in our lives.
they manifest the fruit of
the spirit to us, and those
moments continue to speak
to our hearts years later.
i remember times when you manifested the fruit of
the spirit. times when you . . .

♦ showed me Love when i felt no one cared ♦ gave me
joy because of your smile and cheerful laughter ♦
blessed me by sitting quietly together so i could find
peace ♦ extended patience to me when i forgot to do
something i promised ♦ spoke a
gentle word of kindness ♦
were so filled with goodness
that you came to my aid at a
difficult time ♦ blessed me with
your faithfulness when others
turned against me ♦ reached
out to me in gentleness when i
felt overwhelmed ♦ kept your
self-control even though i
lost mine ♦

you are truly a friend of
the spirit.

Kim Lancaster

The Door County Ladies
Bonnie, Linda, Terry, Virginia, and Barbie

LifeLong friendship

S ometimes when my schedule is overloaded, I day-dream about a log cabin in a serene north woods setting—no deadlines, no phone, no pressure. Your getaway dream might be of a beach house, a farm, or the mountains. But, as a former Wisconsinite, I feel more relaxed and in awe of God's creation in a wooded setting with a lake or pond and lots of wildlife. Many special spots in Wisconsin could provide all three of those elements, but my husband and I especially appreciate Door County on the peninsula between the bay of Green Bay and Lake Michigan. At the height of summer, the place is jam-packed with people fishing, swimming, shopping, or waiting in line three-deep for a generous double-decker ice cream cone at Wilson's Ice Cream Shop in Ephraim.

My friend of many years, Virginia Duncan, loves Door County as much as I do. Many years ago Virginia orchestrated fall getaways to the woods of Door County for a group of six she dubbed "The Ladies." We usually drove up in pairs as our schedules permitted. The first two or three to arrive would open the cabin, start a crack-ling fire in the fireplace, and stack dried wood near the hearth. Since we all took turns preparing meals, Friday's chef would begin dinner. Over the next few hours the others would arrive. Some were giddy and keyed up, others worn and in need of a hug. We all were thrilled to be together and looked forward to our weekend of encouragement and rejuvenation.

What a mixed group we were. Some had grown children and grandchildren; some hadn't started families; others had teens; and still others small babies. Some were spiritual, some were not, and some were searching. Some were businesswomen, while some were at home full-time. We came in all shapes and sizes and from different backgrounds. But everyone of us was appropriately awed by the beauty of a crisp fall morning in Door County, trees ablaze and vapor rising off the lake. It was glorious.

The most meaningful times were when we bared our souls and tears spilled as we gathered around the fireplace sharing thoughts and feelings long into the night. Burdens were lifted as we sat around the dinner table laughing and commiserating over our shortcomings and challenges. Through the years, we helped each other weather marital problems, rebellious teens, financial crises, and personal loss. We laughed together, cried together, learned from each other, agreed to disagree, and made allowances for each other's shortcomings.

The Ladies continued to meet for a while after I moved south. But, eventually, Virginia Duncan moved out west for part of the year, and over time the distance between us grew. Virginia still keeps us all posted on each other's families, activities, and well-being.

But I feel a little nostalgic when I think about what we once experienced together, and knowing the season for these rendezvous has passed. I'm a richer person because of that season in my life when The Ladies—Virginia, Linda, Bonnie, Barbie, Judy, and myself— offered each other comfort and encouragement, laughter and tears, refreshment and renewal. It was a splash of joy this side of heaven.

Authors have written books and producers have created movies about friendships that have been kept alive and nurtured because of ongoing rendezvous. As so many of the stories in this book confirm, in a time of need, nothing is so appreciated as a friend. Even our times of celebration become twice as meaningful when we share them with someone who rejoices with us.

Our God created us to be relational—first with Him and then with each other. As He pours Himself into us, we are to let His presence and His power flow out to those around us. We are meant to give and to receive. Friendship requires both. Really special friendships require putting the other person's needs and concerns above your own. It's been said that in order to have a friend, you must first be one.

If you've gotten this book for yourself, I hope as you've read it you've felt gratitude for the special friends with whom you've been blessed. If you've been given this book by a friend, it's an acknowledgement of how much you mean to her. In the busyness of our world and the clutter of so much "stuff," take time to invest in each other.

Celebrate your friendship. Cherish your friendship. Nourish your friendship by getting together with old friends and contacting those childhood sisters you haven't seen for years. In the overall scheme of things, life is brief but people are eternal.

✦ ✦ ✦

"Intimate friendship provides us with a picture of
what awaits us with God in Heaven."
—Unknown